Never
Mind
the
Zombies

Books by Pat Anderson

NOVELS
The McGlinchy Code
The Crimes of Miss Jane Goldie
Torrent
A Toast to Charlie Hanrahan
Catalyst

FACTUAL
Clash of the Agnivores
Fear and Smear
Never Mind the Zombies
Yellow Peril
Rattus Agnivoricus
Up to Our Knees

FOR CHILDREN
The Skyscraper Rocket Ship
The Ceremony at Goreb Ridge
The Brain Thing
The Football Star
Mighty Pete and the
School Bully School

Never Mind the Zombies
Here's the Agnivores

THE RETURN OF
THE REAL RANGERS MEN

Pat Anderson B.A. P.G.C.E. F.H.S.I.B.

Snowy Publications MMXVII

First published 2015

This edition 2017

Dedicated to all the Internet Bampots

Contents

Contents

Preface

Smugness isn't one of the Seven Deadly Sins but it's probably bubbling just under those top malefactions. There's nothing worse than a smug bastard, smile on his face, telling everyone how he was right all along. Unfortunately, smug is the only way to describe how I feel now. While everybody concentrated on finances and the like, I had my finger on the pulse of The People.

All the bedsheet-wavers, the Sons of Struth, the Rangers Supporters Trust and the rest weren't interested in millionaires, billionaires and warchests, front-loaded or otherwise. All they wanted was to see Real Rangers Men back in charge at Ibrox.

Phil Mac Giolla Bhain and other commentators now accept this theory, even though it seems to make no sense. But, then, when did The People ever make sense? And who was the one that first put forward the idea that all most of The People cared about was Real Rangers Men?

Anyway, enough of all this smugness or I'm going to put you off reading the book. Oh, go on – just one more: I told you, didn't I?

This book covers the period from where I left off in 'Clash of the Agnivores', summer 2014, to summer 2015. You might think you already remember everything but so much happened during that time that I found myself surprised while researching. I would read a newspaper article and be amazed; was that really only six months ago?

As usual I have tried my best to balance out the need for historical accuracy with making the book enjoyable. Hopefully I have succeeded in both respects. Again I've decided to employ a more informal way of writing, which I hope makes the book less of a dry read.

Any quotes I've used are verbatim, including mistakes with spelling, grammar and syntax. I've corrected one or two where it was necessary to understand what was said, so any mistakes aren't mine! (Unless, of course, they're in the actual text – my copy of Word is stuck on US English when correcting, so a couple of Americanisms might have slipped through.)

My usual thanks to all the Internet Bampots that have supported me and to all those that follow me on Twitter. And, of course, to everybody that reads my blog.

Apologies to Monti. I had said that this book would be shorter, and therefore cheaper, than 'Clash of the Agnivores'. It looks, however, as if it's turned out just the same length. Monti seems to have recently become Scotland's version of Bear Grylls, so he might not have time for reading books! But, then, my wife hasn't read a single one of my books, so he's in good company!

And my usual special gratitude goes to Shaun, who supported by blog right from the start, and, of course, Mick, without whom I'd probably still be counting my sales in single figures.

So here's Volume 2 of the Ibrox saga. I hope you enjoy it!

Pat Anderson
July 2015

Introduction
Pretty Vacant

When we left our intrepid heroes they still hadn't managed to get Real Rangers Men into the boardroom. They were determined, though, and Honest Dave King had organised a 'trust fund' for The People to put their season-book money into, instead of giving it to the 'spivs' and 'crooks' at the top of the marble staircase.

The second part of 'The Journey' was over, with Neo-Gers winning Division 2 quite comfortably. The general consensus, however, was that Sooperally's team was shite and that a lot of improvement was needed. Nevertheless, that didn't stop The People and the agnivores in the media being bullish about the coming season in the newly-formed Championship. They were coming down the road again and everyone was apparently terrified of a resurgent 'Rangers'.

As far as The People were concerned, the old club/new club debate was over. The SFA, the SPFL, UEFA, the UK Government, the EU, the United Nations and God Himself had announced that the club was 'still Rangers'. Anybody that said otherwise was an obsessive and a bigot. And then one Donald Findlay Q.C. put in his tuppence-worth.

The interview given by Findlay to the Daily Mail came in November 2014, well into the new season and well after the beginning of this book. It does, however, sum up the theory I put forward in Clash of the Agnivores and which I still hold to in this book. It's worth quoting Findlay at length:

> It is a different club. They may play at Ibrox and they may play sometimes in royal blue jerseys. But you cannot pass on that which is undefinable. And that is spirit and tradition and all the rest of it. To me this is a new Rangers which has to establish its own history and tradition. But it's not the Rangers
> I know. To me, genuinely, it is a new entity.
> Well, the view I have is one expressed to me by a lot of other

Rangers supporters. There is just not the same sense of things being done the Rangers way. A lot of Rangers supporters – and these are the guys I feel sorry for – paid their money and remained loyal and followed the team through thick and thin. And they tell me there is just something missing now. That's not only my view. It's what I am told by people from the inside in the sense that they go to Ibrox. Something has changed, something is missing. It's just somehow… different.[1]

Of course, there was a backlash against Findlay, with much wailing and gnashing of teeth, including a rebuke of sorts from Sooperally;[2] but, deep inside, The People knew he was right. There was something missing; something that would have made their contention that it was 'still Rangers' more secure. This missing something was what they had been fighting for from the moment Charles Green started up his new club: Real Rangers Men, all brogues, blazers and bigotry, in charge in the Blue Room. Everything else was secondary.

Never Mind The Zombies

Image courtesy of Kittisak at FreeDigitalPhotos.net

1
God Save The Queen

On 19th April 2014 Neo-Gers brought on a substitute in their game against Stenhousemuir at Ochilview. The game was already won by the time this substitute came on; Neo-Gers were up 3-0 and there were only about twenty minutes to go. It was a good time to give a run-out to a youngster knocking on the door of the first team.

Charlie Telfer had signed for Rangers when he was eight years old and had been at Ibrox ever since, through all the changes. He was a bright prospect, having already won caps for the Scotland U-17 and U-19 teams. This was his first ever appearance for the first team and, no doubt, he hoped to impress enough to be picked again.

Kyle Hutton sang Telfer's praises, saying, 'All he needs is to make a few more appearances and get his confidence up and that will be him.'[1] But would he get the appearances he needed while Sooperally was manager? Some of The People certainly didn't think so. As one of them said, '…why stick with a club where youth are never given a chance and we sign has-beens?'[2]

The rumours were flying around in May that Telfer was offski; the story was that he was going to sign for Dundee United. And, of course, the stories turned out to be true. At the beginning of June Charlie Telfer signed for Dundee Utd, rejecting a deal with Neo-Gers. He said, 'I have watched how the younger players at United are allowed to develop in the first team, and that has been a big reason in my decision to join the club.'[3] He might as well have said that he had left because youth didn't stand a chance at Neo-Gers.

Graham Wallace had outlined in April that there were going to have to be cutbacks; but allowing up-and-coming players to leave surely wasn't what he had in mind. The People, understandably, were incensed; Sooperally should be building for the future. Unfortunately, it still hadn't occurred to them that they, themselves, were the problem.

In 'Clash of the Agnivores' we looked at how the Big Lie left everyone's hands tied. An integral part of believing that this new club

1

was 'still Rangers' was getting 'back to the top where they belonged'; and the sooner the better seemed to be the demand. So rather than gradually build up a team to rise through the leagues, adding to it as they went along, Sooperally, and the board, had to make sure that Neo-Gers steamrollered its way to the top tier. The People would accept nothing less.

Not that Sooperally's team had been an overly effective steamroller; it had actually struggled at times when winning the bottom two tiers. Yes, Neo-Gers were way ahead of the rest of the pack in terms of points but they had stuttered and stumbled their way through most of their matches to get there. Quite often they had had to rely on a penalty or the sending off of opposition players to attain victory. It did not bode well for life in the Championship, especially since Hearts and Hibs were going to be there as well. It was obvious that a bit of strengthening was going to be needed.

Ally, however, seemed to let his heart rule his head. True, there was no money to buy players but surely he could have got some out-of-contract young players, or even a couple of loan signings? Instead, he decided that Real Rangers Men trumped any thought of building as strong a team as possible and signed Kris Boyd and Kenny Miller.

To be fair to Boyd he had lost weight and worked on his fitness since the days he had left Rangers; his stint at Kilmarnock in season 2013-14 had actually earned him a nomination for Player of the Year. He still, however, had the same problem he always had; a distinct lack of pace. Walter Smith had never rated him as a team player but as somebody that might get a goal when things weren't going too great. Sooperally was taking a huge chance here.

He was taking an even bigger chance with Kenny Miller, a man that makes Madge in 'Benidorm' look peely-wally. Miller had never really lived up to the promise he had shown in his younger years and was never the prolific goalscorer he should have been. His major strength, unlike Boyd, had always been his pace but he was now in his mid-thirties; would his legs still be as good?

Cynics accused both men of simply looking to top up their retirement funds; a claim that was rubbished by the media. There was a case to be made that Boyd wasn't in this category; he had shown at Kilmarnock that he was a man with a point to prove. Miller, however, was another matter.

Much was made of the fact that Miller was getting less of a salary 'than deals given to players such as Sebastien Faure and Arnold Peralta by former chief executive Charles Green.'[4] He had also given up a massive salary with the Vancouver Whitecaps to come to Neo-Gers. But he had wanted to leave the Whitecaps anyway; he said, 'The club wanted to go in one direction, I wanted to go in another direction.'[5] This, however, was bending the truth more than a little.

The fact was that the Whitecaps didn't want to pay Miller's inflated salary anymore since he was no longer as fast as he used to be. He didn't actually have a choice in the matter; he was out the door whether he wanted to stay or not.[6] So his move to Neo-Gers was possibly not the great act of altruism that he was making it out to be. Not, of course, that our Fourth Estate would be contradicting him any time soon!

Whether or not Miller and Boyd were getting as much as Peralta had got, the fact remained that they were hardly going to be on minimum wage. Their salaries were an extra burden; on that was going to have to be offset by cuts elsewhere.

A few players' contracts came to an end in summer 2014 and could be taken off the payroll. There were not as many for the chop as most of The People would have liked but that was something that couldn't be helped. Many players only signed up to play in Division 3 because they had been given long-term contracts that would probably take them into the higher tiers. Neo-Gers couldn't get rid of these players without having to fork out hefty severance payments.

Despite still being encumbered with a lot of dead weight, not to mention Ally's bumper salary, the board was bullish about the future. There were plans to raise about £8m with another share issue to institutional investors in London.[7] The Chief Executive, Graham Wallace assured the supporters that all was well, saying, 'The long-term financial stability of the business is well in hand and we are in a good place now.'[8]

He then played the old Charles Green 'victim' card to get all The People onside. He said:

> There are many non-Rangers fans who support other clubs and who are genuinely concerned about the progress we are making and the momentum we are building. They know where we're headed and they'd just love for us to falter. We're not going to allow that to happen. [9]

Things, however, had moved on a good deal since Green was handing out cups of tea. It wasn't other clubs' supporters that were worried; it was a sizable portion of The People themselves.

Remember Honest Dave's Trust Fund, with Richard Gough coming on board to persuade The People not to buy season tickets? The Real Rangers Men supporters kept demanding to know how many season books that Neo-Gers had sold so far and, finally, the board acquiesced. By the middle of June the figure was 17,000; exactly half the number that had been sold the previous season.[10] Obviously the board needed cash badly or administration beckoned. There were big salaries to be paid, as well as the two outstanding loans. The share issue seemed to offer the only way out.

To those of us on the outside looking in, this share issue, with shares being sold to those that already held sizable amounts, appeared ridiculous. Incredibly, it involved diluting the value of shares already owned, meaning that an investor would have to fork out cash just to hold the same percentage of the company he already had. It's one of the vagaries of the way business works and is usually a last-ditch effort to keep a company going. Shareholders would have to decide whether to pump more money in to keep their holding viable or face the prospect of owning shares in a dead company. Essentially, it was a question of passing the hat round.

The Easdales, along with Graham Wallace, attended various meetings in London to persuade investors to go along with the scheme.[11] Shareholders would have to agree to the issue before it could be done. Not only was the board planning to pass round the hat; they wanted investors to lend their hats for the job.

But that wasn't all. Share issues usually require an underwriter, somebody that will pick up the shortfall if the issue ends up being undersubscribed. You might remember that underwriting the Rangers share issue helped to seal the doom of David Murray's regime when The People kept their hands in their pockets. Would anyone be willing to take the chance of underwriting this particular share issue? After all, investors might see it as a good idea but then expect other shareholders to be the ones to stump up the cash. If nobody actually put their money where their mouth was then it could turn out to be a costly business for the underwriter.

Blue Pitch and Margarita, the mysterious investors whose proxies the Easdales held, appeared to be up for injecting more cash into the business,[12] which meant that it might be easier to persuade others to part with their money. Without an underwriter, however, the whole thing would have to be called off if not enough investors subscribed. It could end up just being an expensive waste of time.

Rather perversely, it was how Neo-Gers was going to do on the pitch that would make the difference to raising finance or not. Normally, the poor showing of Ally's team was blamed on all the off-field bickering in the boardroom; now it was the team's chance to show its mettle and make Neo-Gers appear a worthwhile investment. This had all been part of Wallace's master plan, after the famous 120-day review. Neo-Gers would storm into the Premiership in 2015 and then be Scottish champions by 2017. The team would then show the big boys of Europe what was what.[13] It sounded more like *Mein Kampf* than the projected future of a football club!

If the Neo-Gers board was bullish about the upcoming season the media were slightly less so. The general consensus was that Neo-Gers would win the Championship but it wasn't going to be as easy as their last two title wins. (As if folk couldn't have figured that one out for themselves.) Everybody, though, was bullish about one thing: the Championship was going to be the most exciting league in Scotland next season.

The story was that the Premiership was boring and that Celtic would walk it easily; a bit of a slap in the teeth for the other teams involved! They might as well just declare Celtic Scottish Champions on the first day of the season and then let all the other teams fight it out for second place. The Championship was going to be far more competitive and all the focus was going to be there.

> In the second tier of Scottish football for the 2014/2015 season you have the two biggest teams in Edinburgh in Hearts and Hibs, who have won the Scottish league eight times between them, and Glasgow Rangers, 54 league titles, Cup Winners Cup winners and UEFA Cup 2008 runners-up, are playing Championship football. There's no point re-spewing what caused these great clubs to fall to this level, but the Championship is going to be one heck of a good league next year.[14]
>
> The Scottish Championship 2014/15 – The Division to Be In.[15]

> With Hearts, Hibs and Rangers, Next Season's Scottish Championship Will Be Mouthwatering.[16]

5

Potentially, the second tier in Scotland will see a higher average attendance than its top flight, which would not paint a positive picture of Scottish football to viewers looking in.[17]

To read the way they were building things up you would imagine that people were flocking to snap up season tickets and television companies were queuing up to broadcast Championship matches, while ignoring the Premiership. When it came right down to it, though, no matter how it was dressed up, whoever won the Championship was still twelve places below the Scottish Champions. It was the second tier and there was no disguising that fact.

Season ticket sales at Hearts might suggest that observers were correct in their analysis; by mid-July Tynecastle had already sold more than they had the previous year.[18] This, however, could well have more to do with the club being more stable than it had been the year before. The sales were probably helped too with the season books being cheaper if you bought them before July 14th.[19] The situation at Hibs could not have been more different.

By the middle of July Hibs had only sold about five-and-a-half thousand, and most of those had been bought before Hibs lost the play-offs against Hamilton.[20] For some weird reason the Hibs Chief Executive, Leeann Dempster thought it was a good strategy to maintain season-ticket prices at the same level as the year before.[21] The Hibs fans were not exactly happy about paying the same money to watch their team play Alloa and Cowdenbeath as they had to watch Hibs against the likes of Celtic, Aberdeen and Dundee United. Tales of an exciting, competitive league made no difference to their opinion.

Of the other teams in the Championship, Dumbarton reported increased sales[22]; Falkirk[23], Raith Rovers[24] and Alloa[25] all reported increases as well. There was no shouting from the rooftops from Queen of the South, Cowdenbeath, or Livingston but, no doubt, there was a higher uptake at these clubs too. Perhaps there was something in all the excitement the media was trying to generate after all!

The fact is, however, that increased sales at these clubs might look great when viewed as percentages; bald figures were another matter entirely. Raith Rovers, for example, were boasting on their website at the end of May about 'Early Bird' sales being up 'a massive 35%'.[26] In raw numbers, though, this amounted to the grand total of 1,094 season books.[27] It says something when this club was pleased about this, while

Neo-Gers was upset about *only* selling 17,000!

The media might be building up the coming season in the Championship as the best thing since sliced bread but, in reality, the fans looked like they were going to be staying away in droves. A couple of thousand Raith Rovers supporters turning up at Ibrox were not going to make up for all those unsold season tickets. Such figures were hardly going to make the Neo-Gers shareholders overly keen to buy into the master plan either!

While the board was desperately looking for cash, Sooperally was signing up the cast of Dad's Army and all the King's men were looking to put Rangers together again, the Bogeyman decided to put in an appearance and frighten the life out of everybody. Enter stage left one Charles Alexander Green; the last person anyone expected, or desired, to see.

Charlie, and his big Yorkshire hands, had apparently taken some time off from his French chateau in order to have a go at getting his club back. He claimed to be rounding up investors to buy out all the current shareholders and take his rightful place back at the top of the marble staircase.[28] All those that were fighting to get Real Rangers Men back into the Blue Room immediately reached for the toilet paper. Many a pish-stained bedsheet had gone into driving Green out of Ibrox; surely all that sleeping on bare, soggy mattresses hadn't been in vain?

They might all shout that Green was a spiv and that he'd 'dooped' and fleeced everybody but the truth of why he was so hated was simpler than that: he was a reminder that Rangers had been liquidated. The Big Lie had succeeded in practically tip-exing the 'L' word out of the whole story; the last thing anybody needed was Green turning up to bring the truth back to the fore.

Bill McMurdo, of course, welcomed the possible return of Green; he had always been his biggest cheerleader. It seemed, though, that he still didn't understand what the battle over Neo-Gers was all about. He said:

> Whatever you say about him, Charles Green is a rainmaker who can bring revenue and funding to Rangers. No wonder those who wish to hinder Rangers in financial and footballing terms hate him so much.[29]

This was a recurring theme on McMurdo's blog; he and his followers were constantly claiming that everybody, including the agnivores in the media, was trying to stop Neo-Gers from progressing. To their fevered minds King, Gough, the media and the whole of Scottish football were colluding with Peter Lawwell to keep Neo-Gers down and leave the field clear for Celtic to win title after title.

The reality was, though, was that it was all about the perception of the Ibrox club. The Union of Fans and the rest all wanted to believe that the new club was 'still Rangers' but it was hard with all those unfamiliar faces sitting in the boardroom; not to mention the hidden faces of Blue Pitch and Margarita. Only the restoration of Real Rangers Men at Ibrox would make it more believable that Rangers had never died.

The battle had been won the previous Christmas but the war was ongoing between the board and the Real Rangers Men. They might all be haunted by the appearance of Charlie Green but, in the grand scheme of things, he was merely a sideshow. There were far more serious things to be worried about come the new season.

In the meantime, Ally and his team were heading for a couple of pre-season glamour ties against Buckie Thistle and Brora Rangers. They were then heading off for a short tour of North America,[30] no doubt staying at various youth hostels on their travels. The rest of us were left to the far less important matters of the World Cup, the Commonwealth Games and a certain referendum.

The World Cup didn't concern Neo-Gers in the slightest. Arnold Peralta was originally picked for the Honduras squad but was eventually ruled out with a thigh injury; well, training with Lee McCulloch does carry a government health warning! As for the referendum, although the likes of McMurdo might shout about how The People were duty-bound to vote for the Union, the truth was that everyone would vote the way they wanted and football clubs weren't getting involved. For The People, though, the Commonwealth Games was a different matter entirely.

Glasgow Council were playing up the whole 'legacy' angle of the Games; you know the kind of stuff – regeneration, jobs, new housing and the rest. There were plans to refurbish and regenerate Bridgeton, Parkhead, Shettleston, Dalmarnock, Rutherglen and Shawfield; areas that badly needed it.[31] Whether or not these plans would materialise was neither here nor there as far as The People were concerned; all they saw was the refurbishment of Celtic Park and they weren't too happy about it.

As early as March a character called Colin Shearer sent this request to

Glasgow City Council:

> How much is the council spending on getting Celtic Park ready
> for the commonwealth games and how much is being spent on
> getting Ibrox Stadium ready for the commonwealth games?[32]

This is couched in terms that make it look like some angry council-tax
payer wanting to know how much of his hard-earned is being spent on
football stadia; a search of the site, however, reveals that Mr. Shearer has
also inquired about collecting tins for 'terrorists' outside Celtic Park. It's
easy to see, therefore, what his real interest is. It's worthwhile too
clicking on the 'Similar Requests' part of the website (What Do They
Know). A quick perusal shows requests about land deals between GCC
and Celtic, questions regarding Celtic season-ticket holders on
committees and even a request asking about any GCC functionaries that
were invited to Celtic's UEFA Cup final!

If you have read 'Clash of the Agnivores' you'll already know what all
this stuff was about. Many of The People were determined to somehow
prove that Celtic had been in receipt of 'state aid' from Glasgow City
Council. Even members of the Democratic Unionist Party in Northern
Ireland were involved in these endeavours. Despite their best efforts,
however, nothing had been proven. They had managed, though, to get
the European Commission involved and a preliminary inquiry was
already underway.

The use of Celtic Park for the Commonwealth Games opening
ceremony was, to them, the last straw. In their eyes it proved the big
conspiracy that had supposedly involved Celtic getting land on the
cheap. They awaited the results of the EC inquiry with ghoulish
anticipation. In the meantime they were faced with the prospect of the
Queen, *their* Queen, opening the Games at Celtic Park. It didn't bear
thinking about!

McMurdo and his contributors, of course, were in the forefront of the
condemnation. McMurdo himself got the ball rolling.

> I am hearing that Mr Lawwell has far more say in the running of
> these Games than could be considered appropriate but no doubt
> this will be put down to sour grapes. Events of the past few years
> have seen Rangers being persecuted in what has to be arguably
> the worst witch hunt in modern Scottish society, while Celtic

have enjoyed preferential status with the nodding acceptance of the so-called Scottish Government.[33]

The ones that posted comments on his blog were equally as scathing, if not more so.

...and then when you see the line-up of singers, rod fucking stewart, that other crackpot susan boyle, it's a tim fest, all we need are the ice cream sellers with the funny hats and the line-up is complete. I hope it rains every fucking day and it's a wash-out.[34]

...can anyone tell me where the regeneration of Hampden, Mount Florida, Kings Park and Toryglens happening?[35]

Either this last character is being disingenuous or he's never been to the places he's talking about. Mount Florida has always been a rather well-to-do area, which is reflected in the price of property there. King's Park, meanwhile is also full of owner-occupied properties and I doubt said owner-occupiers would be best pleased at suggestions that their neighbourhood needs regenerating! As for Toryglen, efforts have been going on for years to regenerate the place; the large sports centre next to Holyrood School, the jobs provided by the Asda superstore and Prospecthill Circus being pretty much transformed, to give just a few examples.

The real concerns of The People are expressed in another post on McMurdo's blog.

I recently paid a visit to Govan town centre and was appalled at the deriliction and abject and how this corupt Glasgow council has syphoned off funds to pay for the "regeneration" of the east end.at the expense of Ibrox and Govan.[36]

I used to work in Govan and I was constantly appalled at the way folk vandalised their surroundings. The school I worked at had money thrown at it hand-over-fist and had facilities that other schools could only dream about. The pupils abused and ruined everything around them, a crowd of them even spending one playtime smashing all the glass on the front doors. The bus station at Govan Cross was always being smashed up; often in broad daylight. Anyone that visits Govan can see that efforts have been made to improve the area, while the local neds continue to do their best to make the place look like a pigsty.

At any rate, for all their moans and groans, there was nothing The People could do to stop Celtic Park receiving a facelift. After all, it wasn't just the council that was involved; the Scottish Government, the Westminster Government and the Commonwealth Games

committee were all in on it as well. Were they going to claim that the UK Government and the whole of the British Commonwealth were conspiring to aid Celtic? They were going to have to wait for the EC report to find out.

And so, as the new season beckoned, The People did not exactly have their troubles to seek. Their club had no money and was relying

on old crocks to get into the Premiership, the support was divided about the way forward, Charlie Green was back, putting the Big Lie in jeopardy and, to top it all, Celtic Park was receiving a make-over that would leave Ibrox looking even more like a crumbling cesspit. And the Queen was coming to Glasgow to witness it all! Who'd be a Neo-Gers supporter, eh?

2
I'm Not Your Stepping-Stone

The new season started for Neo-Gers with a third stab at the Challenge Cup, now sponsored by Petrofac Training and called, imaginatively enough, the Petrofac Training Cup. After making it all the way to the final last season, only to be beaten by Raith Rovers, Sooperally and his team were determined to get their hands on the trophy this time. Their first-round match was against Hibs at Ibrox on 5th August.

Neo-Gers won the game 2-1, with the Hibs goalscorer, Danny Handling being sent off in the 79th minute, when the score was still 1-1.[1] It was interesting to see how the media reacted to the sending-off. The Daily Record called Handling's foul a 'horror tackle on David Templeton',[2] while the Edinburgh Evening News said that the red card was a 'harsh decision'.[3] Everyone agreed that Handling was sent off during a period of Hibs superiority; nobody, however, bothered to draw any conclusions from this. If they had they would have realised that Neo-Gers were perhaps not the world beaters they were being made out to be.

Things on the money front weren't going too great. The intended share issue turned out to be a complete disaster. It was seriously undersubscribed and, with no underwriter, the whole thing had to be abandoned.[4] The plan now was for a reduced issue to all shareholders with a reduced target of £4m.[5] They were still, however, looking for an underwriter. If Ally's team was successful on the park then it would make the whole business a lot easier.

Neo-Gers' opening match in the Championship was a Sunday fixture at home to Hearts. Although everybody said it was going to be a close match, they expected Neo-Gers to emerge triumphant. Hearts had spent most of the previous season fielding youngsters; it was all they could afford in their dire financial straits. Surely they wouldn't have a chance against experienced pro's, like Miller, Boyd and McCulloch? (No sniggering at the back, there!)

As it transpired things went awry for Neo-Gers. There's no need to

12

mention who won; let us simply say that Sooperally's team came in second.[6] To say Ally wasn't too happy was putting it mildly. In the 'Rangers' spirit of dignity, accepting defeat and moving on, Ally looked for people to blame. He whined about Hearts taking centre before the Neo-Gers sub, Darren McGregor, was on the pitch,[7] but his ire was mostly directed at Charles Green. Charlie had appeared in the press on the Friday before the match, reiterating his intent to raise cash from investors in order to take over Neo-Gers again.[8]

> Whether Green comes back or not we don't know. It remains to be seen. We don't know what's happening but the timing of it, again, wasn't great. For the first time one or two of the players actually mentioned to me about the timing of it. Everyone does their level best to keep players sheltered away from it and we will continue to do that. The only thing they can have a bearing on is results on the park and that's what they have to concentrate on. But sometimes it is just a bit of a sideshow we can do without.[9]

This was Ally's take on how Charlie had affected Neo-Gers, with the players not able to concentrate on their game for looking behind them in case the bogeyman got them! The Daily Record's Keith Jackson pretty much agreed with Ally and put the boot into the Neo-Gers board for good measure.[10] This had become a recurring theme in the Record, which had been against the incumbent board since the 2013 AGM.

The board had more than enough things to worry about to get its knickers in a twist over Green's insane power plays or the constant vitriolic attacks against it in the Daily Record. Again, nobody seemed to be willing to underwrite the new share issue. The desperation of the board in this respect was shown at the end of August when they had to go crawling to the enemy, in the shape of Dave King, to ask him to act as underwriter.[11] After discussions, King refused; no doubt they wouldn't let him get his own way.

King was obviously a last resort and before approaching him the board exhausted every possibility. One of those possibilities was already a shareholder at Neo-Gers, owning 4.56%, and was a billionaire to boot; he seemed the ideal candidate. This was Mike Ashley, owner of Sports Direct, whose company was already in a partnership with the club's retail division. There were rumours that he wanted the naming rights to Ibrox as a quid-pro-quo for underwriting the share issue.[12] Whatever the truth of the matter he evidently did not agree to underwrite the issue; why else would the board have approached King?

To date, Ashley had not been a big player at Ibrox; at least, he hadn't pushed himself into the limelight. Sports Direct had its partnership with Neo-Gers Retail and that was it. Nobody speculated about what Ashley might be up to; as far as could be seen, he wasn't up to anything. King, on the other hand, was a different story entirely.

Those that supported the board suspected that King was intent on causing another insolvency event at Ibrox; possibly even another liquidation. King would then be able to step in and do exactly what Green had done; pick up the assets for a song. We would then be presented with a Neo-Neo-Gers, masquerading as still the same club but with a 'Real Rangers Man' in charge to help maintain the illusion. Even if Neo-Gers didn't become insolvent, there was no denying that King's shenanigans were driving down the share price.[13] This was all part of his plan, according to the board's supporters.

And it certainly looked that way. For all his noises about taking over and coming to the rescue, King had, so far, not purchased so much as one share. His 'Trust Fund' idea was starving Neo-Gers of much-needed cash, as well as frightening the hell out of investors. His refusal to underwrite the share issue seemed to point to this conclusion as well; after all, he would have ended up a shareholder if the scheme was undersubscribed, which was more than likely, given the past record of The People in such circumstances. Obviously he had no wish to become a shareholder; not yet, at any rate.

As August wore on and made way for September the need to rally against King and the Real Rangers Men became more and more apparent. The board and its supporters needed a champion and they looked increasingly to Mike Ashley to take up the mantle. He wasn't going to underwrite the share issue and there were problems about him owning too many shares, due to SFA regulations, but he was the board's only real hope. He also happened to be a real billionaire; not an 'off the radar' one like Craig Whyte. As Sandy Easdale said in an interview with Keith Jackson, 'who wouldn't want a billionaire investing in their club?'[14]

Bill McMurdo and those that posted on his blog, too, began to pin their hopes on Mike Ashley. The problem, however, was that 'we have no idea what the Sports Direct owner's plans for Rangers are – or if he has any at all.'[15] And this was the problem that everybody had with Ashley; he never let anyone know what he was up to, or even if he was up to anything at all.

In June 2000 Ashley attended a meeting at the Cheshire mansion of one of his rivals, David Hughes, chairman of the Allsports chain of sports shops. Also present was Dave Whelan, chairman of JJB Sports, one of the biggest sports chains in the country. Nobody knows exactly what happened at the meeting but it was something to do with discussing the price of replica football shirts; price fixing, in other words. Whelan supposedly told Ashley, 'There's a club in the north son, and you're not part of it.'[16]

Ashley might not have been part of the club but it's a reasonable assumption to make that he was being asked to join; why else would he have been there? Whether he was being invited to become a member or not, Ashley took at different route. He grassed up the lot of them, sparking a huge investigation and massive fines for those involved.[17] It was certainly some way to sort out your rivals!

Then again, the whole idea of price fixing was anathema to Ashley, whose sales philosophy was pile 'em high, sell 'em cheap. Even major brands were often used as loss-leaders to entice folk into his stores, where they would find a cornucopia of previously unavailable goods. His ownership of Donnay, Dunlop Slazenger, Lonsdale and Karrimor meant that he could sell such brands cheaply but still show a massive profit. It also meant that he could put these prestige labels on things like tracksuits for toddlers.[18]

He was an intensely private individual, never attending functions and never giving interviews. In the mid-2000s nobody had even seen a photograph of him, prompting Philip Beresford, who compiles the Sunday Times Rich List, to call him, 'Britain's answer to the late Howard Hughes'.[19] It was even said that many of his own staff didn't know what he looked like.[20] This meant, of course, that rivals couldn't read him or know what he was about.

Then there was the strange story of JJB Sports. From a position of being Britain's biggest sports retailer the company went into administration in October 2012. Ashley snapped up fifty of JJB's stores, as well as the Slazenger Golf brand and even the company's Wigan headquarters.[21] So what went wrong?

JJB had been in trouble for years, narrowly escaping administration in early 2009. At the same time the company admitted to the Office of Fair Trading that they had been involved in price fixing with Sports Direct the previous year. The company's chairman, Sir David Jones, secured immunity from prosecution for JJB for giving evidence.[22]   The alleged price fixing had apparently taken place under the previous chairman, Chris Ronnie, whom Jones had subsequently driven out.

During his almost two-year tenure, Ronnie was the one that started all of JJB's financial troubles. He was installed as boss of the company after buying 29% of the shares. His purchase of two smaller retail businesses for JJB, Qube and Original Shoe Company, was a disaster. Both Qube and OSC lost money hand-over-fist[23] and JJB never recovered.

It is interesting to note that Ronnie formerly worked for Ashley and was still a friend. Also interesting was the fact that Ronnie bought Qube and OSC from, you guessed it, Mike Ashley. It could all, of course, be a massive coincidence but, it has to be said, Ashley was the main beneficiary of the collapse of JJB. He hasn't looked back since. Chris Ronnie, on the other hand, ended up with a four-year prison sentence for accepting back-handers from suppliers when he was running JJB.[24]

Ashley was obviously not a man to be trifled with and was someone that was determined to do business in his own way. His experience at Newcastle United FC, where he was initially a high-profile 'saviour' of the club, only to be castigated by the fans when things went wrong, had probably influenced his decision to remain in the background at Neo-Gers.

The main allegation thrown at Ashley by NUFC fans is that he lacks ambition. Initially, the entry of a billionaire onto the scene sparked hopes that the glory days of the mid-nineties, when NUFC was challenging Manchester United for top spot and Kevin Keegan had his much-publicised feud with Alex Ferguson, might return to St James's Park. Within two years of Ashley's takeover, however, the club was relegated to the Championship. They won promotion at the first time of asking but, ever since, the club has been static in the middle of the Premiership table.

Ashley's main concern at NUFC seems to be in making a profit and in advertising Sports Direct. In recent years NUFC has become a club that nurtures talent and then sells it on for a profit, rather than signing big names to mount a challenge. Indeed, in January 2015 NUFC was listed as the 19th richest and most profitable club in the world.[25] And yet the club has consistently been going nowhere as far as challenging for honours is concerned. No wonder the Newcastle supporters are so pissed off!

To the supporters of the Neo-Gers board, however, it was going to be different at their club. It doesn't seem to matter what happens, or what blatant truth presents itself to them; The People have a remarkable ability to delude themselves. Whether it's a convicted criminal or a hard-nosed businessman they're following, they'll just shut their eyes, put their fingers in their ears and shout down anyone that tries to tell the truth about their hero. They are gulled time and time again because they cannot comprehend anyone knowing better than they do.

And so it was with Ashley. McMurdo and his fellow travelers convinced themselves that he was going to be their saviour, even though the man himself gave no indication of being any such thing. His reluctance to underwrite the share issue was explained by McMurdo as the fault of the SFA. Ashley had been keen to get involved but the SFA had stopped him due to their rules about dual ownership of football clubs.[26] Even Sandy Easdale got drawn into the wishful-thinking scenario in his interview with Keith Jackson, claiming, 'His (Ashley's) plan was to increase his shareholding but he's come across a stumbling block with the SFA.'[27] Earlier in the same interview, however, he had said, 'He basically *may* have a plan to put into place.'[28] (My italics) In other words, Sandy had no more idea of what was going on in Ashley's mind than anyone else.

The Daily Record, as the champion of the Real Rangers Men, also bought into the idea that Ashley might be ready to take over at Ibrox. The reaction of the Record hacks was predictable: paint Ashley in as bad a light as possible. Strangely, they ignored all the stories of his previous business dealings and what had happened at

Newcastle United; no doubt they realised that The People wouldn't believe such things. Instead, a story emerged that would strike fear into the heart of any Rangers-cum-Neo-Gers supporter.

In his interview with Keith Jackson, Sandy Easdale let slip that Ashley already held the naming rights over Ibrox. He refused to say how much Ashley had paid for this, but he made it plain that Sports Direct

> have a predetermined contract which was agreed before any of us got there. If Mike Ashley was of a mind to then he could call it the Sport Direct Arena tomorrow. But he's obviously not of a mind to because it's two years in and he's not doing it at the moment.[29]

As if that wasn't bad enough, Keith Jackson revealed that Charlie

Green had actually sold the naming rights to Ashley for the grand total of one pound! Charlie then spent £250,000 in legal fees trying to get the contract annulled; but it was watertight.[30] Phil Mac Giolla Bhain, in a rare instance where he was second to Jackson on a story, put the figure for the legal fees closer to £400,000.[31]

Of course, this had the desired effect; The People were incensed, especially the Real Rangers Men contingent. The Daily Record's Hotline gave some examples:[32]

Ashley would do well to remember that is was Ibrox then, Ibrox now and it will be Ibrox forever.

Mike Ashley can forget all about renaming the stadium.

If Ashley is wise he will never invoke that £1 naming rights clause.

Strangely McMurdo and the other supporters of the board didn't question these figures. The figure of £1 seemed to have been conjured up from nowhere with no proof whatsoever. The fact that nobody at Ibrox came out to dispute what Jackson had said perhaps points to it being true. Then again, this was Ashley we were talking about and he wasn't about to divulge anything. Even those closest to him on the board had no idea what he was planning, as subsequent events would show.

It was only a day or two after these revelations that another shock was announced. All the staff in the 'Rangers' stores, at Ibrox, at Glasgow Airport and in Belfast, were now Sports Direct employees.[33] The board tried to put a positive spin on it:

All other retail functions including our online store and warehousing are currently operated by Sports Direct. Outsourcing the retail element of a football club's operation is a common practice within the industry and is a positive move.[34]

The Real Rangers Men side was unconvinced. Craig 'Halloween' Houston said, 'I don't think there will be too many people using that business.'[35]

At any rate, the division in the Neo-Gers support had found respective figureheads. The Real Rangers Men side were still placing all their trust in Dave King, even though the man was a convicted crook.

The supporters of the board, meanwhile, were putting all their hopes onto Mike Ashley's shoulders, despite the fact that Ashley appeared unwilling to take up the mantle. Rather weirdly, King owned no shares whatsoever in Neo-Gers, while Ashley only held 4.6% and seemed in no hurry to buy any more, SFA rules permitting or not. They appeared unlikely generals in the war for Ibrox; but both were being thrust into that position by The People and the press. A billionaire versus a (presumed) millionaire; who would win out?

3
<u>My Way</u>

To the surprise of nobody the share issue failed to reach its target of £4m. In fact the money raised was just enough to get the issue limping over the finish line. With no underwriter the whole thing would have had to be abandoned, and money returned, if the take-up was less than £3m. As things turned out £3.13m was raised,[1] bringing a sigh of relief from the Neo-Gers board; albeit a temporary one. George Letham and Sandy Easdale were still to get their loan money back; plus interest in the case of Letham. That £3.13m wasn't going to last very long!

More money disappeared from the pot when Imran Ahmad finally received his long-awaited payoff. It was announced that he received 'significantly less' than the £620,000 he had been demanding but he certainly must have got a six-figure sum or he wouldn't have been willing to settle. The Real Rangers Men contingent was not best pleased about this, especially since Neo-Gers had already spent money fighting Ahmad in court.[2] Chris 'Ze List' Graham was incensed and voiced his anger to the press, saying, 'If they are expecting an easy ride at the AGM then I can tell you they'll be sorely disappointed.'[3]

Outside of this internecine feud the biggest talking point was the fact that Mike Ashley hadn't bought any shares. Both sides of the Neo-Gers divide reacted to this differently. McMurdo was bitterly disappointed.

> As readers of this blog know, Mike Ashley was seriously considering a greater involvement at Ibrox but it now looks like he has done an about face on this – understandable, given the hostile climate created by the malcontents at the club.[4]

Those 'malcontents' were strangely muted. They might have been expected to be crowing triumphantly over Ashley's reluctance to be the hero of the current administration but, instead, they kept their own counsel. No doubt they suspected that Ashley was up to something.

They would have been right.

On October 1st it was reported that French bank, BNP Paribas, had bought 5% of Neo-Gers from investment managers Hargreave Hale for £850,000.[5] Hargreave Hale originally paid the best part of three million quid for its shares, so it was taking quite a hit. This could be viewed in two ways: either as rats deserting a sinking ship or as great news that a huge concern like BNP Paribas was investing in Neo-Gers. We only had to wait another day to find out the truth of the matter.

It turned out that the French bank had not bought the shares on its own behalf; it had been acting for a client. That client was Michael James Wallace Ashley, who was now the second-biggest shareholder at Ibrox with 8.92%.[6] The big question was why he hadn't bought the shares in the share issue. Obviously he had some reason for not wanting his cash to go straight to the Neo-Gers board; it was a strange one.

The whole business of Ashley's involvement in Neo-Gers was becoming more and more mysterious. The SFA has supposedly strict rules about owning stakes in two separate clubs but, not surprisingly, these rules were bent to breaking point to accommodate Neo-Gers. Ashley was allowed to buy shares but was told that he had to stay under 10%.[7] There were UEFA regulations to adhere to as well but, then, NUFC and Neo-Gers were hardly likely to face each other in Europe anytime soon!

Apparently the Neo-Gers board asked the SFA's permission, in September 2015, for Ashley to up his stake to 25%. The SFA, instead of turning them down flat, asked for a business case for this idea; Neo-Gers never got back in touch.[8] Obviously whatever Ashley had been planning, he changed his mind. More likely, he had just been weighing up his options before committing himself. As usual, nobody had any idea what the hell Ashley was going to do.

McMurdo had got himself a bit overexcited back at the start of September with the news that Ashley was putting Newcastle United up for sale.[9] If he had bothered to look into things he would have known that this was news that Newcastle supporters were fed up hearing. Twice before Ashley put NUFC up for sale, only to withdraw it when nobody suitable came forward.[10] This time was no different and it was only a day after McMurdo's excited ramblings that Ashley made it plain that Newcastle United was not for sale; not yet anyway.[11]

Ally's team, meanwhile, had picked itself up after the opening-day loss to Hearts. They won their next four Championship matches convincingly enough and looked to have gained momentum until they only managed to scrape a draw away against Alloa. The Daily Record, however, was quick to explain this 'blip' as being caused by the poor, artificial surface of Recreation Park.[12] Not so easily explained away was the drubbing meted out by Hibs at the end of September. There were even calls for Ally to quit.[13]

Looking on the bright side, though, Neo-Gers were still in all three cup competitions; even seeing off Premiership side Inverness Caledonian Thistle in the League Cup. Yes, they had been lucky, a deflected shot beating the Inverness keeper and Inverness having a goal chalked off for offside, but they were still there.

October continued to be good for Neo-Gers on the pitch, with a 6-1 drubbing of Raith Rovers helping to restore a bit of pride. They also managed to keep progressing in the cup competitions, even claiming another Premiership scalp in the League Cup in the shape of St. Johnstone (although the solitary, winning goal by Lewis Macleod looked suspiciously offside). Financially, though, things were looking decidedly shaky and there was even a rumour that soon there wouldn't be a club to progress anywhere.

It didn't take Alan Turing to figure out that Neo-Gers were facing a cash crisis. With a sharp decline in paying customers and the money from the share issue going to pay off loans and Imran Ahmad, they needed some source of finance and fast. There was, however, a bit of a dispute in the board room about where this money should come from.

Graham Wallace, the Chief Executive, and Phillip Nash, the consultant that had been brought in to save the club, had been having discussions with Dave King, Paul Murray and George Letham (yes, the man that had helped out with the loan) about some kind of multi-million-pound bail out.[14] Ashley wasn't overly keen on these discussions and even called for an EGM to get Wallace and Nash booted out.[15] He still gave no indication of what his own plans were.

On 14th October, King arrived in Scotland to meet with the Neo-Gers board along with George Letham. They emerged full of confidence that their proposals were going to be accepted, getting the Daily Record all excited in the process.[16] The Real Rangers Men were coming down the road!

The terms of King & Co's financial largesse, however, was not calculated to win over the current shareholders. They were offering

22

sixteen million quid, a tidy sum, but, in return, they wanted a new share issue, whereby they would get 51% of Neo-Gers.[17] This would considerably reduce the holding of those that currently held a stake in the club; but it could be argued that a small piece of something was preferable to a large piece of bugger all!

As it turned out, much to the chagrin of many of The People, the board knocked back King's offer. The reasons were not given out immediately, but Phil Mac Giolla Bhain pointed out that if King's consortium bought, or acquired, 51% of Neo-Gers then, under Stock Market rules, they would be required to bid for the other 49%. According to Mac Giolla Bhain, King just wasn't prepared to do this, ending all discussion on the matter.[18]

The Neo-Gers chairman, David Somers, later told a different story. Apparently, King and his cronies could provide no proof of funds, meaning that Somers couldn't recommend their proposal to the board. Nor were they prepared to divulge who the other five members of their consortium were. This meant, Somers said, that he couldn't carry out due diligence;[19] a check that must have come as something of a novelty in the Blue Room!

Whatever the given reasons for knocking back King's offer there was one, more obvious reason for not letting him in the door. The man is a convicted criminal and any sane person wouldn't trust him to put a line on at the bookies for them, let alone take over their football club!

An insight into Ashley's plans came with the story that he had demanded ownership of the club's trademarks, including the Rangers crest, in return for a loan to see them through the financial crisis. According to Keith Jackson, Wallace and Nash both blocked this in the boardroom; this explained why Ashley was so keen to have them removed.[20] It was also, possibly, the reason why he had refused to have anything to do with the share issue; he wanted the club vulnerable so he could get his own way.

Once King's offer was safely killed off, Ashley was in pole position with another loan offer. His terms were that he wanted Wallace and Nash out and his own men appointed to the board.[21] It looked like the Real Rangers Men had failed yet again. Then, to the intense relief of Keith Jackson and the rest of the brown-brogue brigade, another messiah appeared on the scene.

Brian Kennedy, the owner of the Sale Sharks rugby club, had

attempted to come to the rescue before, way back in March 2012.[22] He had been a reluctant saviour, promising to buy Rangers only if the administrators couldn't find anyone better. Of course, as we now know, Duff and Phelps already had their backstairs deal with Chateau Charlie lined up and Kennedy wasn't needed or wanted. This time, though, Kennedy wasn't offering to buy anything.

It was difficult to see how Kennedy's offer of a loan of £3m was any better than Ashley's reported offer of about the same. Nobody doubted that Ashley's loan would come with strings attached; he already had a good chunk of the retail income in his pocket and the fear was that he wanted more. But what did Kennedy want? Rich men don't give away money for nothing, unless they're getting old and ready to meet their maker. Whatever Kennedy's terms were, we weren't told; he was going to stop Ashley and that was good enough for the Real Rangers Mens' supporters.

It was only later that we discovered what Kennedy's demands actually were. As well as Edmiston House and the Albion Car Park being put up as security, he also wanted Ibrox stadium placed in some kind of trust so that no loans could be raised on it.[23] The board probably had no problem with this; after all, it was perfectly reasonable for a creditor to have some kind of security. It was more likely his other terms that caused the board, and, indeed, the shareholders, to think twice. He outlined what his proposals had been:

'Paul Murray to be appointed to the plc main board for a period of 24 months,' he said, adding that the loan 'was designed to give the board of Rangers PLC the time to pursue Dave King's offer and/or a new share issue in order to ensure long-term financial security.'[24]

It was hardly surprising that his offer was rejected; it looked, to all intents and purposes, as if he was just acting as a front for Dave King.

Meanwhile, King's inside men knew that the game was up. While Kennedy was outlining his proposal to the board, Graham Wallace decided to go off on a family holiday. This, apparently, had been arranged well beforehand but it also pointed to Wallace admitting that his influence in the boardroom was gone.[25] Nash, on the other hand, just handed in his resignation,[26] obviously not wanting to give Ashley the satisfaction of firing him.

Dave King had the following to say about Nash's resignation: 'He is a man of integrity. Perhaps he wanted to disassociate himself from something unsavoury.'[27] By God, that's like Sooperally calling Mike

Ashley 'Fatso'!

And so, Ashley's loan of £2m, with the promise of more if needed, was accepted. Not everyone was upset at this turn of events by any means. One commenter on a newspaper forum said, 'Yesss! wee bheelers crying about billionaire Ashley taken control of the Gers can't beat it!'[28] (I've corrected an obvious typo in this post but left the rest as it was.) McMurdo, of course, was cock-a-hoop, as were his followers. The future was beginning to look brighter.[29]

Those rather obvious exceptions aside, however, The People weren't happy at the outcome. The cries of 'spivs' and 'crooks' were heard once more and the smell of pish-stained bedsheets filled the air again. These folk weren't going to back down until the Real Rangers Men were in the Blue Room.

Already, at the end of September, the Sons of Struth were calling for a boycott of Sports Direct and McGill's buses.[30] Obviously they hadn't properly thought that one through. In Inverclyde McGill's buses has a virtual monopoly, so if you don't want to use that company's vehicles the only alternative is to walk. As for boycotting Sports Direct; what were their kids going to wear to school? The plan was pretty much a non-starter.

Bizarrely, the final straw for the Sons of Struth apparently came when Sandy Easdale was pictured meeting Rafat Rizvi, a man wanted by Interpol and who had been convicted of fraud in absentia by a court in Indonesia.[31] It seemed that the Sons of Struth didn't want a convicted fraudster getting involved with Neo-Gers... At any rate, the Sons of Struth gave Ashley an ultimatum: give up the naming rights to Ibrox or else! No doubt Ashley's bowels were quivering in fear.

Of course, these demands were ignored so the Sons of Struth took their protest a step further. On 11th September they targeted Sports Direct and Cruise shops, demonstrating outside and disrupting business inside. Their wizard wheeze was to take a pile of expensive goods to the checkout and then offer a pound, the same amount Ashley reportedly paid for the naming rights to Ibrox.[32] Oh, how we all laughed at this jolly jape! Many of the People weren't too impressed by the stunt, though the Sons of Struth patted themselves on the back for a job well done.[33] It is noteworthy, however, that they never repeated this operation.

The Rangers Supporters Trust decided not to opt for such juvenile pranks but instead formed its own company, Fleshers Haugh, to sell

25

rival clothing to the official, Mike Ashley, merchandise.[34] The colours chosen were red and black, the colours of the old Govan Burgh and they were going to avoid using anything that might infringe on any club copyrights. They had big ambitions, asking for anyone with experience in design and manufacture, as well as marketing to come forward to help.[35] All the money raised would be used to buy shares in Neo-Gers.

Their ambitious plans, however, seem to have come to naught. As of July 2015 the Fleshers Haugh website is still 'under construction'.[36] There are a couple of links to buy merchandise, but all that's available are red and black scarves and red and black tops. A stumbling block might well be that the shirts only go up to size XXL,[37] which is probably too small for the average Neo-Gers fan that we see on television. The official top, on the other hand, goes up to a roomy XXXL for a replica home shirt,[38] while a replica third shirt can be had in a whopping XXXXXL size![39] A family could probably live in one of those.

These black and red scarves and shirts had been on sale since 2012 to raise money for the Rangers Fans Fighting Fund and quite a few had been bought. You might remember, however, that a lot of The People turned against the RFFF when it emerged, in March 2014, that some of the money was going to be used to pay for Craig Houston's defence against Sandy Easdale's intended legal action.[40] This was hardly going to get folk rushing to snap up the items a few months later. Certainly Mike Ashley wasn't going to be losing any sleep!

As we've already noted, not everyone was desperate for the Real Rangers Men to take over Neo-Gers. We had the commentator in the Scotsman cheering on Ashley while McMurdo and his crew constantly beat the drum for him. As Sandy Easdale had said, it made sense to be happy about having a real billionaire on board. As we have seen, however, there were plenty that weren't. The funny thing was, though, that the pro-Ashley and anti-Ashley sides were both worried about exactly the same thing.

It's been pointed out on many occasions that it was obsession with Celtic that caused the demise of Rangers. Claims of being the 'world's most successful club' were laughable while Rangers had never won the big one: the European Cup. Celtic, of course, had achieved this feat in 1967 and it has stuck in the collective craw of The People ever since.

Sour-grape stories about the trophy not being worth as much back in the 1960s, fewer teams competing and the match officials in Lisbon 'cheating' in Celtic's favour were no help. Complaints from The People and the media that Scottish football was doing nothing to help Rangers in Europe were laughed at and were compared to Celtic's achievement in winning all domestic honours in the same year as winning the European Cup! Even when Rangers put five dummy stars on their jerseys it didn't help; everyone in Scotland and beyond knew that the single, solitary star on the Celtic jerseys was far more prestigious.

Since everyone was pretending that the new club was still Rangers, the obsession with Celtic continued unabated. The fear that Celtic might achieve ten in a row and surpass the record of 54 league titles held by Rangers was palpable. The People might try to console themselves by saying that Celtic's achievements would be somehow tainted but that would make not one iota of difference to the official statistics. Somehow Neo-Gers was going to have to be built up to present a challenge to Celtic. All The People were agreed on this; the big divide was over how this was to be achieved.

Those that supported the Real Rangers Men had been unhappy ever since Chateau Charlie appeared on the scene. You'll remember that they tried to get him out before he'd even set foot on the marble staircase and nothing had happened to change their minds since. It didn't matter how much money the owners of Neo-Gers had; they weren't Real Rangers Men so the club wasn't the 'Real Rangers'. An important part of being the 'Real Rangers' was obsessing over what was happening across the city. Only a 'Real Rangers Man' could understand this obsession.

At the end of 2013 David Leggat was vocal in his belief that everyone connected with Celtic was terrified of Dave King and the rest of the Real Rangers Men taking over. Unfortunately, most of his blogs have disappeared so I can't direct you to his exact words, only what I reported in 'Clash of the Agnivores'.[41] All the rhetoric from the Sons of Struth etc. in the last quarter of 2014 still showed this obsession with Celtic and the Real Rangers Men mounting a realistic challenge. As one of The People commented, 'The fear of the return of Dave King to Ibrox is delicious to observe.'[42]

The truth was, however, that nobody connected with Celtic or its support was in the least bit troubled by the possibility of a convicted criminal taking over at Neo-Gers. Surely it was of more concern that a real billionaire was in charge? To the fury of The People, however, nobody was particularly bothered about Mike Ashley either. It seemed that no matter who was going to be in charge at Ibrox there was a distinct lack of perturbation over at Parkhead.

The big question is why. Why did nobody see a threat to Celtic from a Neo-Gers run by a billionaire? It's time to have a closer look at Mike Ashley and his probable plans for Neo-Gers.

4
No Feelings

There is a book called 'The Rise and Fall of the Third Reich', by E.L. Shirer that gives an interesting account of Nazi Germany. A lot of historians can be quite snooty about the book; Shirer was a journalist, not an historian. Certainly some of Shirer's historical conclusions are a bit suspect, such as his argument that anti-Semitism was a legacy of Martin Luther. That aside, however, the book gives an excellent, first-hand narrative of the rise of Nazism and the early years of World War II. Shirer was actually based in Berlin in the 1930s and was there right up until America entered the war in 1942.

One of the recurring themes in Shirer's book was his surprise at how everyone was apparently taken unawares by Hitler's moves, like the Anschluss with Austria and the annexation of the Sudetenland. Everything that Hitler did had been set out in *Mein Kampf* and one only had to look at what he had already done to see what he was going to do. He was pursuing the old *Grossdeutschland* approach of the Nineteenth Century, as well as the *Lebensraum* policy of the Kaiser's Germany. Shirer was amazed at how nobody could see the logic and sheer transparency of Hitler's actions.

Similarly, nobody seemed to be aware of Mike Ashley's plans, even though they were there for all to see in his tenure at St. James' Park, or the Sports Direct Arena, as it was known for nearly a year.

We have already looked at Mike Ashley and there is a recurring theme evident in all his dealings; the main concern of Mike Ashley is......Mike Ashley. Everything he has done at Newcastle United has been for the benefit of Ashley's company; why should things be any different at Ibrox?

Even a cursory glance at St. James' Park these days shows that it is mainly a vehicle for advertising Sports Direct.[1] We have already discussed how the NUFC supporters are incensed at the lack of ambition shown by Ashley and his board; honours come a distant second to profits and the club's directors seem content for Newcastle to sit mid-table from now until doomsday.

E.L. Shirer would find it amusing to see the way that McMurdo and his followers closed their eyes to what was happening at NUFC. One of the members of Team McMurdo had the following to say:

> Mike Ashley is manoeuvering and positioning himself at Ibrox. Why? Does he see this as a glaring opportunity to make money? Absolutely! But can Rangers become a Champions League Club in the near future under his stewardship? Definitely![2]

He goes on:

> Mike Ashley has a proven track record in business – crucially, although he is hugely unpopular on Tyneside, he has steadied the ship there. I believe Newcastle are in debt to him, deep debt at that, but I believe if he was offered the right amount, he'd walk. Which would leave him free to snap up Rangers – and a way to get his Sports Direct signs all over Europe, at a tiny fraction of the cost in comparison to Newcastle.[3]

This character was actually outlining what Ashley had done at Newcastle but seemed convinced that he would, for some strange, unspecified reason, behave completely differently at Ibrox. This delusion even extended as far as believing that Ashley would want to get Neo-Gers into Europe, even though he had studiously avoided such a scenario at St. James' Park!

In reality Ashley would have nothing whatsoever to gain from Neo-Gers taking part in European competitions. UEFA has strict regulations about advertising and only UEFA partners and sponsors are allowed. If Neo-Gers, or NUFC for that matter, were to get into the Champions League or the Europa League then all the Sports Direct adverts would have to be removed. Why on earth would Ashley want that? Even allowing for the fact that getting into Europe from the Scottish Premiership is a less costly proposition than it is in the EPL, it would still be a waste of money as far as Ashley was concerned.

Ashley had already shown by his reluctance to buy shares in the share issue that he was not there to pump money into Neo-Gers. His *modus operandi* was to lend money to the club, with assets like the Albion Car Park being demanded as security. Anyone with eyes could see that he intended to do at Ibrox exactly what he was doing at St. James' Park.

Phil Mac Giolla Bhain speculated even further, a few months later, that it was possible that Ashley didn't even want to run Neo-Gers. The club was running at a loss and the stadium was going to need a fortune spent on it; who needed the hassle? Much better to let someone else have the headache while Ashley continued to cream off the revenue from the retail sector.[4] He would also be there with a loan whenever it was needed; after all, who else would they be able to turn to?

Phil Mac Giolla Bhain could well have been right. Ashley was already involved in a club besides Newcastle and Neo-Gers; Oldham Athletic. He didn't buy any shares or anything; he simply signed Oldham up to a sponsorship deal with Sports Direct worth £1m over five years. In a rare positive piece about Ashley, the Daily Record had Lee Johnson, manager at Oldham, waxing lyrical about what a great deal it was for the club.[5] Oldham was now able to build a long-awaited new stand and the hope was that they would now be able to fight their way up to the Premiership.

So what did Ashley get out of it? Well, as usual, he put his advertising boards everywhere, had the name of his company on the team's shirts and even renamed Boundary Park; it was now called Sportsdirect.com Park. Integral to the new stand was going to be the club shop, run by Sports Direct, of course, who would pay sales royalties to the club.[6] That all sounded rather familiar and was guaranteed to cause a shiver of fear up the collective spine of The People.

This is what Phil Mac Giolla Bhain, or, rather, a business analyst of his acquaintance, envisaged was Mike Ashley's plan, not only for Neo-Gers but for any other club he could get his hands on. Providing loans and tying up the retail sector seemed to be the way to go.[7] In this scenario Ashley would try to offload Newcastle United onto somebody else, as he had always promised he would. And even if he did sell it, the club apparently still owed him £130m and he has the retail revenue sewn up.[8] No doubt those retail contracts are airtight and will continue no matter who owns the club. It's hardly surprising that no buyer has come forward yet!

It would seem, then, that all the pishy-bedsheet wavers were right in their assessment; Ashley wasn't going to be doing their club favours any time soon. The problem was that it didn't look as if they would fare any better with the Real Rangers Men *in situ* either.

In March 2014 Dave King had estimated that bringing Neo-Gers up to scratch was going to cost about £50m over four years. He claimed that he, personally, would stump up £30m of that if he managed to take over the club.[9] Of course, things didn't go his way so he never had to put his hand in his pocket.

By the time October came around, the money that King was offering had reduced considerably. As you'll remember, this time he was going to *lend* Neo-Gers £16m and not all of it was his own money. Apparently he was unable to provide evidence of any funds, which makes one wonder where that thirty million quid disappeared to!

Not that King was going to get the chance to show how much money he had anytime soon; Ashley seemed determined to stop anyone coming in to move this cash cow out of his milking shed. It looked as if Phil Mac Giolla Bhain's assessment was wrong and Ashley wanted to stay in control.

And so we moved into November. Ashley loaned the club another million on top of October's £2m, tightening his grip further but giving up the right to rename the stadium.[10] No doubt the latter was a sop to the bedsheet wavers in the hope that they'd either give up or piss off.

Meanwhile Derek Llambias, one of Ashley's associates, was appointed to the Ibrox board, as per the conditions of the loan.[11] Another Ashley associate, Barry Leach, was installed as a consultant[12] and would no doubt be given a seat in the boardroom before too long; Ashley's contract entitled him to two appointees.

With all that settled it was time to have another look at Graham Wallace's much-vaunted 120-day review and see what cuts could be made. Sooperally, his staff and his players were all on watertight contracts; the Ibrox ancillary staff, however, was not so fortunate. Ten folk were given their marching orders, some of whom had worked at Ibrox for decades.

Gordon Waddell, in the Sunday Mail, banged on about what a disgrace it was, especially as it came only a few weeks before Christmas.[13] Funnily enough, I don't remember Waddell shedding any tears about all the folk that were left out of pocket when Rangers was liquidated! No; it was just fingers in the ears and pretend that the new club was still Rangers.

Waddell took issue with Ian Black, who had said about the financial situation at Ibrox:

32

The only time it affects you is when it gets to the stage when you're not getting paid. That's the only time it will affect the players. Until then we don't really pay attention to it.[14]

Waddell found this to be an absolutely disgusting attitude. A bit like the callousness shown to all the creditors when the Big Lie swindle was perpetrated! Amazingly, Waddell called this lack of empathy and sympathy 'Ashleyfication', as if it was something new at Ibrox. Tell that to the wee face-painting woman!

He went on to compare the attitude of Celtic supporters, who were currently lambasting their club's board over paying staff a living wage. He certainly had a point. While Celtic blogs at the time were up in arms about staff earning a decent wage, Neo-Gers supporters had a completely different attitude.

One blogger, for example, had this to say about Laura Tarbet, a woman we shall hear more of later, who had been at Ibrox for forty-three years:

Well, excuse me…if I don't shed a tear for her; it sounds as if she's had a decent living out of Rangers for all those years. Plus she must be near retirement age already so no big deal. With the current state of the club's finances she's exactly the type of person who should be getting the chop, hopefully to make way for a much cheaper 20 year old to take over her duties.[15]

Well, that certainly showed that Waddell was right but was this a new phenomenon? Waddell seemed to think so but, then, he had the Big Lie to maintain and 'Rangers' being taken over by heartless spivs and crooks was an integral part of that. Surely he can't have forgotten that charity money being siphoned off into Rangers?[16]

There was also another important matter that Waddell deemed to be not worth mentioning while he shed blue-tinted tears over these folk that lost their jobs. In the late 1980s it used to make me sick to my stomach when I was out drinking in Edinburgh's New Town and some middle-class tosser in fancy dress would shove a tin in my face, expecting me to give generously for Children In Need. As I told them, in no uncertain terms, maybe if they stopped voting for Thatcher and supporting her cuts in taxes and cuts in welfare we wouldn't have any children in need! And the same goes for Rangers before liquidation.

Waddell praised all the great charity work that Rangers have been involved in in the past but, just like those individuals in Edinburgh, this needed to be weighed up against the tax money, or lack thereof. While raising money and giving money to charity, Rangers, at the same time, was avoiding paying its fair share of tax. Did the charity cash match, or surpass, the tax that Rangers didn't pay? Somehow I doubt it. Those charitable acts, therefore, are indelibly tainted. The non-payment of tax also shows that selfishness and lack of caring did not suddenly arrive at Ibrox with Mike Ashley!

Sooperally expressed his sadness about what was going on at Ibrox, saying:

> We definitely are now missing people that have meant so much to Rangers over the years. It's extremely sad to see people go, very good people, great people. I couldn't name them all, but Laura, for example, has been here with the Rangers for 42 years. She was on the flight to Barcelona. The first manager she worked for was Willie Waddell, so that woman, in my opinion, deserves to have her name on the board going up the stairs at Ibrox.
>
> She should be in the Hall of Fame. It is natural when you lose people like that it affects you and saddens you. There's no use shirking the issue. We don't have John Greig any more, we don't have Sandy Jardine, we don't have Laura Tarbet. It's sad we're losing people that are synonymous with and have an identity with the club.[17]

Even though our eyes are all misted up we should still see Ally's sob story as part and parcel of the Big Lie. All this stuff about the heart being ripped out of the club was really only relevant if we accepted that the club was still Rangers. Sooperally had never made any secret of the fact that he was on the side of the Real Rangers Men and his tale of woe was a direct challenge to the current board.

He mentioned Laura Tarbet, a woman, as we saw earlier, who had been at Ibrox for forty-three years. If someone like her wasn't safe, then who was? Her dismissal was also an indication that Ashley and his men weren't in the least bit interested in keeping up the pretence of continuity. Whether or not the club was 'still Rangers' wasn't their concern. As long as there were supporters to keep buying the replica strips then they could call the club whatever the hell they wanted.

The Big Lie might not have been important to Ashley and his associates but to The People and the Scottish media it was all they had to cling onto. A world without Rangers in it was enough to drive them into a cold sweat so the pretence had to be maintained at all costs. It's time to look more closely at how the Big Lie operated and how it was cynically manoeuvred to operate always in the interests of the club at Ibrox.

5
Liar

Although Mike Ashley and his associates couldn't care less about the Big Lie, the fact was that it was necessary if The People were to keep buying the merchandise. Despite all the hoo-ha in the Daily Record about red-and-black scarves and suchlike the vast majority of The People still wanted to wear 'real' Rangers stuff, no matter who was selling it.

And so the Big Lie continued, even though it meant continued support for the Real Rangers Men in the media. It was a delicate balancing act that Chateau Charlie, the Easdales and everybody else that had got their feet under the table in the Blue Room had to perform: pretend that the club was still Rangers but downplay the need for Real Rangers Men in the boardroom. When it came to forking out money, however, it was a different story entirely.

Neil Alexander signed for Rangers in 2008. Even though he was second-choice goalkeeper behind Allan McGregor, he actually featured in quite a lot of matches. It was not surprising, then, that he signed a new, three-year deal in 2010.[1] None of us was made privy to the details of Alexander's new contract, but we would find out alright when it came to an end!

When Charlie Green started up his new club several players, including Allan McGregor, decided to go off to pastures new. Neil Alexander, on the other hand, decided to participate in the Big Lie and signed up with Green. After all, everyone was adamant that the club was still Rangers and Alexander would now be number one choice between the sticks. All going well, he would still be plying his trade in the SPL as if nothing had happened!

TUPE (Transfer of Undertakings Protection of Employment) regulations are there to protect employees if a company changes hands. The rules are quite explicit in making sure that the new owners fulfil all obligations to employees that were extant under the old owners. It is debatable if TUPE regulations would apply given the fact that Green bought the assets and not the company. Green certainly seemed to believe that these rules applied, even though he had a rather topsy-turvy idea of how they worked. He seemed to think that employees were *obliged* to transfer, even though the rules made it plain that no such obligation existed.[2]

Also made plain was that if an employee did transfer then he carried over the contract he had with the old employers. The actual legislation said that

> all the transferor's rights, powers, duties and liabilities under or in connection with the transferring employees' contracts of employment are transferred to the transferee.[3]

Again, it was debatable whether TUPE applied in the circumstances at Ibrox but Green was making so much noise about such regulations being in force that it would be difficult to deny.

When summer 2013 arrived Alexander's contract was at an end. He refused to sign another deal and, as Sooperally admitted, he wouldn't be at Ibrox for the new season.[4] Why he wasn't staying nobody would say. Maybe he wanted to stretch himself in a higher league or maybe he was just tired of 'The Journey'; we would have to wait until December to find out.

Alexander had wanted to stay at Neo-Gers but it seemed that Charlie Boy made a pig's ear of negotiations. That's when Alexander decided to move on. Being rather pissed-off, to say the least, at the way he'd been treated, the goalkeeper also decided that he might take Neo-Gers to court over parts of his contract that had not been honoured.[5]

Apparently there was a clause in Alexander's contract that promised, on the departure of McGregor, a pay rise and higher appearance fees.[6] Neo-Gers wouldn't stump up the cash while Alexander was at Ibrox, so they were hardly going to pay up when he wasn't. Their argument was that McGregor had not technically 'transferred' so the contract with Alexander wasn't valid.[7]

Eventually, in December 2014, an SPFL tribunal decided that Alexander was indeed entitled to his money and ordered Neo-Gers to come up with £84,000.[8] Neo-Gers straightaway put in an appeal, probably because they didn't have £84,000 to spare. The appeal would be heard by the SFA, where, no doubt, the Ibrox club expected a more sympathetic ear. If not then Campbell Ogilvie might suddenly discover repayment being demanded for that 'loan' he received a while back!

It was difficult to see what kind of argument Neo-Gers could come up with. They've never disputed the contract itself; only the fact that the circumstances of McGregor's departure somehow invalidated it. It is seriously doubtful that Alexander's contract specified under what circumstances McGregor would have to leave, so, effectively, they didn't have a leg to stand on. Their only chance was to argue that TUPE regulations didn't apply and the only way to do that was to prove that Green didn't buy the club! It's an expensive business the Big Lie!

On a side note, it's worth noting the language used in the Daily Record when they reported Alexander's victory. There was no positive case to be made in Neo-Gers' defence, so the Record decided to attack Alexander instead. Apparently he was 'ready to pocket a fortune' after he 'was able to persuade an SPFL panel' of the righteousness of his case.[9] No wonder some of The People were angry at him.

> Fuck off Neil we have made you a millionaire yet you still
> want more prick.[10]
> Ffs.[11]

> He stayed for the fight....then raped us in court for money we
> don't have. Another backstabbing judas.[12]

> This is very disappointing. I know footballers are mercenaries
> but fuck...[13]

One or two saw things more clearly, like this commenter:

> It's complicated as McGregor fucked off but Alexander had a
> contract with us and carried it over so unless we're claiming
> we're a different club I think he's right and due it.[14]

Of course, the Big Lie could come in handy; especially when it came to claiming money. Such was the case with Charlie Telfer, who, if you recall, had turned down a new contract at Neo-Gers to play Premiership football at Dundee United. Since Telfer was a free agent then no transfer fee needed to be paid. There was, however, the matter of payment for the years of development Telfer had received at Ibrox. United offered

£80,000, Neo-Gers wanted £200,000; it was going to have to go to a tribunal.[15]

The size of the settlement, of course, all depended on whatever point of view one took vis-à-vis the Big Lie. If you accepted that the club was still Rangers, then Telfer had been there for ten years; otherwise, it was only a matter of two years. No prizes for guessing which figure the Neo-Gers board, not to mention the agnivores in our media, championed!

It was obvious from the start that United were in for a major disappointment. Our football authorities were just as complicit in perpetuating the Big Lie as the media so they were hardly going to change their minds now. It was not exactly a big surprise, therefore, when the SPFL tribunal ordered United to pay Neo-Gers £204,000.[16]

Stephen Thompson, the United chairman, was absolutely livid and made no bones about the fact that he found the size of the settlement ludicrous. He was careful, though, not to say the wrong thing and face the wrath of the agnivores and our 'impartial' football authorities. Bizarrely, it was Neo-Gers that shot themselves in the foot.[17]

No sooner had the tribunal made its decision than Neo-Gers had the following little tirade on its website:

> Dundee United introduced a late argument stating Rangers should only be awarded compensation for the training and development of Charlie Telfer for two years instead of the 10 years that he was with the Club.
> They argued the club in its current form has only existed for two years.
> It is disappointing Dundee United tried to pursue this tiresome, legally incorrect and provocative argument given that it has been repeatedly confirmed by the football authorities in Scotland and beyond that administration and liquidation of the companies that owned the Club did not break the continuity of the club's history or its record of honours won.[18]

Stephen Thompson, however, had made no such claim at the tribunal; he had far too much sense for that. Dundee United's lawyers were straight on the case and the post had to be removed from the website. Nobody at United had mentioned anything about 'new clubs'; it was Neo-Gers that had inadvertently brought the truth to the fore. Fortunately for them, our compliant media didn't pursue the matter and it was quickly swept under the carpet. There was more danger to the Big Lie to come, though.

It was only a week after the tribunal made its decision that a shock appeared in the media. BDO, the liquidators of the old club/holding company/whatever, were looking into claiming a share of the Charlie Telfer money for the creditors.[19] Now that was really going to stir things up!

If Neo-Gers wanted to claim all the cash for Telfer, then they were going to have to prove that they were the ones out of pocket. That would be impossible. As they never tired of letting us know, it was a different holding company in charge of the club prior to August 2012. If they tried to make out that the club paid out the cash to develop Telfer, then they would have to admit the truth: Rangers was incorporated and Neo-Gers was a new club as well as a new company. There was no way of denying BDO's claim without giving up on the Big Lie!

Clinging onto the Big Lie, however, took a back seat when it came to actually paying out money. Remember Laura Tarbet, the wee wummin that Sooperally claimed should be in the Ibrox Hall of Fame? Well, it turned out that there was more to the story than her simply being booted out of Ibrox, along with others, to save a few bob. It seemed that Mrs. Tarbet was only paid redundancy money for two-and-a-half years; the time she had worked for the new club/company/whatever![20]

Normally, items that appear on Phil Mac Giolla Bhain's blog find their way into the papers, usually in the shape of a Keith Jackson exclusive; this time, however, was different. Yes, it would have provided great ammunition against the Neo-Gers board in the quest for the return of the Real Rangers Men, but it would have put a serious dent in the Big Lie. That was something that none of our agnivores could countenance.

We have already seen how explicit TUPE regulations are, so if Charlie Green had bought Rangers, as the Big Lie said he did, then, obviously, Mrs. Tarbet's redundancy entitlement should have transferred over. The truth was that Green actually bought the assets and started up a new company-cum-club. TUPE regulations would not apply since Mrs. Tarbet had not 'transferred' but had signed a contract with an entirely new business entity. Q.E.D. Not surprisingly, our media just ignored this story.

On the pitch, meanwhile, things weren't going too great. Ally's team continued its record in the Challenge Cup by being beaten 3-2 by Alloa in the semi-final on 3rd December. The calls for Sooperally to go were growing almost as loud as the anti-board protests. Not for the first time, and certainly not the last, the team was booed off the pitch at full-time.

Then, on 12th December, Neo-Gers were beaten 2-0 at Palmerston in a league match,[21] leaving them nine points adrift of Hearts, who had a game in hand. This, however, was not what concerned our media. The big story was that Sooperally had handed in his notice. Neither Ally nor the board would confirm or deny that he was doing 'walking away' but speculation was such that it seemed almost certain. It was the Monday, the 15th, before matters were confirmed by the board informing the Stock Exchange that Sooper had, indeed, resigned.[22]

A few days later, the Daily Record had the headline, 'Ally McCoist on the reasons behind his Rangers resignation'.[23] As usual, though, no difficult questions were asked and Sooper gave nothing away whatsoever about his reasons for going. He did speak, however, about how he wanted to be remembered:

> Everyone will have a different opinion but the only thing that matters is the Rangers supporters felt I did everything for them and the club. That will be the only thing that matters to me. People will have different opinions on my management skills and techniques, but I would hope that even the people who are justified in criticising me would appreciate the mistakes I have made have been honest ones. I've been trying to do my best for the club and hope they realise that. That means more than anything.[24]

This heartwarming speech, however, was somewhat at odds with reality. Ally had been on a massive salary ever since the days of Charles Green and it had never been made clear whether or not the much-vaunted reduction had actually happened. Whatever the size of his wage-packet he was definitely due to receive £750k for his final year in charge. And that wasn't all. Phil Mac Giolla Bhain informed us that Sooper had also had an expense allowance of £125k per year.

This meant that, altogether, Ally had raked in the best part of two-

and-a-half million quid during his time at Neo-Gers.[25]

The People always profess not to believe anything Phil Mac Giolla Bhain says but, even if you discount his information, nobody could possibly argue that Sooperally hadn't done well out of Neo-Gers. The Easdales, in contrast, took not one penny out of the club and yet they were being accused of being spivs and crooks! They're a funny lot, The People!

'Aye, but they Easdales ur mullionaires,' is the obvious answer to that. 'They kin afford tae dae that!' This line of reasoning, however, ignores Sooperally's probable bank balance. He hasn't been out of work since he stopped playing; regular appearances on Question of Sport, frequent stints as a pundit, that long apprenticeship under Walter Smith. God, he even appeared in a movie! There's no way to be entirely sure how much Sooper's worth, but he certainly won't be near a foodbank anytime soon.

But, being a 'Real Rangers Man', Ally was above reproach as far as The People, and the media, were concerned. His managerial skills might leave a lot to be desired but he had done his best, hadn't he? And, apparently, he had had to contend with a tougher task than any other football manager in the history of the sport. Even Matt Busby dealing with the aftermath of the Munich Tragedy didn't come close!

While many of The People were calling for Ally to step down, a new myth began to take shape in the media: everybody else was to blame except Sooperally. Derek Johnstone pointed the finger at the players and pleaded for the board to give Ally time as well as funds to strengthen his squad in January.[26] This, of course, suggests that he had been unable to strengthen his squad so far, due to the parsimony of the board. Keith Jackson continued this theme in the Daily Record:

> …the ongoing financial difficulties which threaten Rangers survival are not McCoist's doing. On the contrary, by keeping the total at less than 30 per cent of the club's annual turnover, McCoist is running one of the most sustainable wage bills at any football club in Britain. On this basis, they ought to be the model of good financial health. That they are wheezing and spluttering and in need of Ashley's life support, is the sole fault of McCoist's superiors.
>
> …he (McCoist) will point an accusatory finger at those inside

his dressing room and he'll jab another at the characters lurking inside the boardroom. At times, he has been let down by each and every one of them.[27]

This kind of thinking appealed particularly to those of The People that had refused to buy season tickets and demonstrated outside every home game. It was the 'spivs and crooks' at the top of the marble staircase to blame for the poor performances of Neo-Gers; poor Ally was just a scapegoat. It was going to take Real Rangers Men, with light-blue and orange blood in their veins to give Ally the financial support he needed.

In reality, however, this is nothing more than a load of pish. Granted, there was no cash available for signing players but Ally seemed to be given plenty to throw about on big wages. Rather than sign promising youngsters that were out of contract, though, Sooperally was more intent on giving his pals a final payday. Whatever anyone's opinion on how good Kris Boyd or Kenny Miller were in their prime, the fact was that those halcyon days had gone. Ally would have been as well signing Bomber Brown; in fact, given his support for the Real Rangers Men, it's surprising that he didn't!

Sooper never made any secret of whose side he was on in the constant battles for power at Ibrox; giving his proxy to fans groups, interviews in the Daily Record etc. Many employees have been sacked for less, so why not Ally? Either the board couldn't afford to get rid of him or he knew too much and they were terrified that he might shoot his mouth off even more than he was already doing. Whatever the reason, he was hardly what you would call an asset.

Yes, the team had won back-to-back leagues but any neutral observer would suggest that it was done in spite of McCoist, rather than because of him. He continually stuck with players that weren't giving a hundred percent and put his players into what were obviously the wrong positions.[28] He would then stand on the touchline, his arms folded, watching the chaos on the pitch. There was no waving of arms, hand signals or changes of tactics. It was if he didn't have the first idea about what he was doing.

More and more of The People were coming to the conclusion that perhaps Craig Whyte's assessment of Ally had been right all along. It looked as if he couldn't manage a shite with a stomach full of syrup of figs! Of course, there could well have been a more sinister explanation.

Since it was obvious to even the supporters that players were out of position, surely Ally, a qualified coach, could see it as well? Was it possible that he was doing it deliberately? After all, Ally's pals, the Real Rangers Men, had talked of 'starving out' the current board. What better way to stop supporters turning up to matches than serving up a pile of shit week-in, week-out?

In his interview with the Daily Record, if you recall, Ally had said that he had 'been trying to do my best for the club and hope they (the supporters) realise that. That means more than anything.'[29] For the Daily Record, and for many of The People, the 'best for the club' was the return of the Real Rangers Men. It is entirely possible, if not probable, that Ally felt the same way. By driving away supporters was he not doing the 'best for the club' by clearing the way for Dave King and his cronies?

Whatever Sooperally was up to, and whatever reasons the board had for not kicking his arse out the door, apart from it possibly getting stuck, the fact was that the money just wasn't available to pay him off. And Ally was going nowhere without his cash. Ashley didn't seem prepared to stump up; loans were all the club was going to get out of him. It was obvious, though, that something needed to be done. The chances of getting into the Premiership looked slimmer by the day; the last thing they needed was Ally continually fucking things up.

And so, to keep Sooper's hands away from the team, the board, on the 21st December, announced that he had been put on 'gardening leave'.[30] This rather cute phrase was a euphemism for Ally sitting about doing nothing while still raking in his massive salary; whether or not he tended to his hydrangeas was entirely up to him.

£750,000 it was going to cost to keep Ally in John Innes compost and Miracle-Gro, but that was a lot less than what he would be due if they got rid of him immediately. As for Ally, he could have saved the club a fortune if he were to forgo any severance payment, as Paul Le Guen had done in 2007. But, as he was fond of telling us, Ally didn't do walking away; certainly not without a hefty pay-off!

6
No Fun

The day after Sooperally was handed his gardening gloves was the day of the AGM, the Annual General Meeting. There were no requisitioners this year so it looked like the supporters of the Real Rangers Men were going to have to content themselves with hurling abuse and threats. It was certainly not going to be a quiet affair.

David Somers, who had managed to cling doggedly to his position as Neo-Gers chairman, got the day off to a fine start by releasing a statement to the press.[1] He claimed that the club would probably have to borrow more money, due mostly to the season-ticket boycott. There was a good bit of truth in that but it was hardly going to quell the anti-board feeling. He was obviously setting himself up for a rough ride at the meeting.

Somers also had a point when he turned on the media, although he used the usual nonsense about all the negativity being 'anti-Rangers'. In reality, the negativity in the media wasn't directed at the club; it was aimed squarely at the board in the interest of getting the Real Rangers Men into the Blue Room.

It sounded as if Somers had been reading Bill McMurdo's blog or as if McMurdo himself had written the statement. The other part of Somers's statement had McMurdo's prints all over it, either directly or indirectly. It said:

> ...because it is clear to me that a stronger Rangers is good for Scottish football, I have been very disappointed to realise that outside of Ibrox, there sadly still exists a great deal of anti-Rangers feeling, perhaps (although I hope not) even in the football establishment.[2]

All of The People would nod in agreement at that particular complaint; after all, they were convinced that everybody had it in for them. The rest of the statement, however, was going to have those pishy bedsheets flapping frantically.

45

The AGM got off to a bad start as boos and catcalls greeted the board as the members went to take their seats. A touch of comedy was provided by the fact that the board members all trooped into a gazebo set up on the pitch, well away from the baying hordes in the Broomloan Stand.[3] (Cue a flurry of jokes on Twitter about Ally the Gardener providing the shelter!) The noise got even louder when Somers tried to give his annual report. He could hardly be heard above the jeering and laughter.

When it came time for questions, Bomber Brown was there to demand assurances that Ticketus, Charles Green and Imran Ahmad were no longer involved at the club.[4] This wasn't all that he had to say, however, and mere written words can't convey the sheer malice in his voice as he spoke over Somers when he tried to answer the questions Brown had posed. He called the Easdales 'two stooges' and welcomed Ashley appointee Derek Llambias, recently installed as Chief Executive, by expressing the hope that he was better than 'the other rats at that table'.[5]

Much to the chagrin of most of the supporters, Somers was dismissive of Dave King:

> I get frustrated with Dave King. I know a lot of you think he is the messiah. The simple reality is that I asked some simple questions because in the past Rangers have done some terrible deals. They were not difficult - the same as I asked to Brian Kennedy and Mike Ashley: show me the money and names of the eight people in your consortium. He didn't do that.
> But the reality is he has cost the club millions of pounds with the season ticket trust and him advising people to boycott season tickets.[6]

That was all probably true but, like his statement earlier that day, was hardly likely to endear Somers to the section of The People clamouring for Real Rangers Men to take over. And, quite apart from his attack on them that morning, the agnivores in the Scottish media were going to be none too happy at Somers speaking about their hero in that way.

The AGM finished with the voting, which went the way of the board as the proxy votes were brought into play. Among the items pushed through was another share issue. Yes, another one. It was only agreed in principle so far but the institutional investors, as

46

well as the ordinary shareholders, must have been dreading it. It wasn't an ideal way to be raising funds.

This would be the third share issue in just over two years. Effectively it meant that if you had bought five percent of Neo-Gers in the IPO in 2012, you were having to stump up cash at every issue just to maintain your percentage share. If you didn't it meant that somebody else might buy shares and reduce your holding. If you didn't take part in any of the share issues you might find that you now only owned one percent, instead of the five percent you had bought in the first place.

A sign that investors were getting fed up was when Resolution 9 was defeated. Resolution 9 was 'To enable the Directors' authority for the disapplication of pre-emption rights.'[7] What that meant in English was that the board wanted to be able to sell shares to outsiders without the permission of current shareholders, and without having to offer current shareholders the same deal. That, it appeared, was a step too far. It would mean shares being diluted without the current holders even having the opportunity to buy them to maintain their present percentage. There's only so much folk will take; especially business folk.

One final piece of comedy from the AGM was provided by Bomber Brown. While he was shouting and bawling about rats and stooges, he also had a go at Somers for not mentioning Sooperally, a man, according to Brown, who 'has gave everything' for the club.[8] As well as betraying his lack of understanding of English grammar, Brown also showed that he could be quite selective in the ones to blame for the financial problems. While eulogising his pal, he seemed to ignore the fact that Ally had bled, and was still bleeding, the club more than anyone!

With Resolution 9, which was more along the lines of Plan 9 from Outer Space, a potential source of revenue for the beleaguered board had been cut off. As they approached Christmas it looked as if the only money available was going to be in the form of loans from Mike Ashley. Either that or they could get in touch with Bob Geldof to put together a charity record.

For The People the AGM had proven to be as much a disappointment as it had been for the board. The same folk were still *in situ* at Ibrox and Mike Ashley had the club in a tight grip. Having

Real Rangers Men in charge seemed like a distant dream; nothing had changed. All they had managed to do was make an arse of themselves with their shouting, booing and abusive comments.

The only thing the anti-board faction had to look forward to now was the SFA's hearing into Mike Ashley's stranglehold on Neo-Gers. It had been earlier in December, around the time of Ally handing in his notice, that the SFA had announced that it wasn't happy with Ashley's influence at Ibrox. Both Ashley and the club were issued with 'notices of complaint' and were ordered to appear at a hearing on 27th January.[9]

While this was obviously good news to the Real Rangers Men supporters, other members of The People were incensed at this development. Our old pal, Bill McMurdo, and his followers saw it as a big conspiracy. He said on his blog:

> Ashley and his team are now having to deal with muck being thrown at him from several directions, including the football authorities, the Rangers-despising media and, of course, his "competition" - the sportswear sellers among the malcontents of the Rangers support. And, of course, those fans of Glasgow's second biggest team who fear an Ashley regime at Ibrox.[10]

It appeared that McMurdo and his mob were never going to change this particular record; Celtic was running scared of a rich Neo-Gers and was pulling strings in the SFA, the SPFL and the media to kill off any chance of Neo-Gers emerging as a serious rival. Strangely, the paranoia of the anti-board faction leaned in virtually the same direction. Doubts were constantly expressed about the 'Rangers credentials' of the Easdales and internet search engines no doubt went into meltdown when confronted with multiple enquiries as to what school Mike Ashley went to.

Another common denominator among The People was that Scottish football needed 'Rangers' in whatever guise and was headed for financial ruin unless Neo-Gers was the dominant force. As McMurdo put it:

> A very valid question in the Ashley situation is: Does the potential investment and involvement of the Sports Direct magnate benefit Scottish football in general by bringing some much-needed

48

revenue to the game? If it produces a healthier Rangers which in turn attracts sponsor and advertiser money, then it is a no-brainer. In the current climate – and in any climate – this matters more than some dumbass rule.[11]

And that summed up the whole problem with the attitude of The People; they were all for rules, as long as they didn't apply to their club. When their club was treated in the same way as other clubs they tended to twist it around to make it appear as if their club was being singled out for 'punishment'. Of course, this paranoia made them convinced that others were breaking the rules and getting away with it; especially Celtic.

We saw in 'Clash of the Agnivores' how The People were getting themselves all in a lather about Celtic supposedly getting preferential treatment in land deals with Glasgow City Council.[12] If you remember, they wrote to the European Commission about this and, as it was duty-bound to do, the Commission looked into the matter. The media barely mentioned it, feeding the paranoia of The People. Still, the European Commission was bound to find out the truth and Celtic would be finished.

The investigation took the best part of a year to complete, which testifies to its thoroughness. Finally, in November 2014, the Commission came to a conclusion. Unfortunately, it was not what The People wanted to hear. The whole thing was thrown out, with the Commission saying that it 'did not see a basis to investigate the matter further'.[13] To say that The People were disappointed would be an understatement. Here are just a few comments from McMurdo's blog on the matter:[14]

The EC have scored a massive, massive Hanley-esque o.g. by burying their heads in the sand over Celtic. We all know they're guilty.

…the clearing of the filth from using state aid by their pals in Europe.

Not surprised with the EU decision, probably a few backhanders flying about!

The EC findings is no surprise

49

On the EU decision I believe appeals are already in! It seems no proper independent investigations may have taken place.

Maybe Celtic gave the EC Commissioner a 'loan', eh? But one has to ask: if the outcome was expected and the European Commission was just a part of Celtic's 'pals in Europe', then what the hell was the point of dragging the Commission into this paranoid game in the first place? It looked, though, that they were determined not to give up. Apparently, they had also dragged Audit Scotland into it and there was still that slim chance that Celtic might be destroyed.[15] And they call others 'obsessed'!

There was one more piece of bad news for The People to deal with before the year was out. Remember the Nimmo Smith report, which The People took as a verdict of 'Not Guilty' and a vindication of the whole EBT saga? One item that they tended to overlook was that Nimmo Smith imposed a fine on the Oldco for using side letters and concealing payments to players from the authorities. The SPFL, however, had decided not to overlook this little matter and, more than that, insisted that Neo-Gers was liable for it. Since the club was constantly skint then there would be no chance of getting the £250,000 anytime soon, or anytime at all for that matter. They decided, therefore, that the easiest course of action would be 'withholding broadcasting money and other sums due to the Club but which are paid in the first instance to the SPFL.'[16]

As the Guardian put it:

> Newco Rangers assumed liability for the liquidated company's football debts when the club's SFA membership was transferred in July 2012 but it was widely thought that the new fine would not affect the current Ibrox regime.[17]

Well they thought wrong, then, didn't they!

The problem for Neo-Gers was that, under the mysterious Five-Way Agreement, they *had* promised to meet all the football debts of the old club. What was more, the SPFL claimed that Neo-Gers officials had signed a 'written agreement admitting liability for the sum due.'[18] Nevertheless, Neo-Gers decided to appeal to the SFA and said that 'the appeal will be pursued vigorously',[19] whatever that meant.

It kind of summed up where Neo-Gers were when they went to Easter Road for their last match of the year. It was the 27th December, two days after Christmas and Neo-Gers gave everyone a late present by getting slaughtered 4-0 by Hibs. Could things get any worse? Well, actually, they could.

Ever since the season started the media had been singing the praises of Lewis Macleod. Like Charlie Telfer, Macleod had signed with Rangers when he was ten years old and, since his emergence into the first team he had made quite an impression. With their usual gift for hyperbole, the Scottish media already had him up there with

Eusebio, Pele, Maradona, Messi and Ronaldo, even though he was

only twenty.

The People were in two minds about Macleod. Given the way the media were going on about him then he could be sold for gazillions during the transfer window; and Neo-Gers could certainly do with the cash. On the other hand, if they were to get into the Premiership they were going to need players like Macleod. Miller, Boyd and McCulloch were hardly going to cut it in the top league, were they?

On the 31st December it was announced that Macleod was on his way to Brentford, an English Championship side, for 'an undisclosed fee'.[20] Of course, the transfer window wasn't open yet, so he wouldn't be on his way until January 3rd. Twitter was buzzing with jokes about how little was probably paid for Macleod and

about why he hadn't been signed by Manchester United or one of the European giants. The People, however, could console themselves with the fact that Championship clubs in England had a hell of a lot more money to spend than the likes of Celtic. Surely Neo-Gers wouldn't let go of their best player for a pittance?

Hogmanay also brought some good news; well, good news if you were part of the Real Rangers Men faction. Laxey Partners, the Isle of Man hedge-fund company, had sold its shares in Neo-Gers to Douglas Park, George Letham and George Taylor for about £2.7m.[21] The latter three were given the rather cuddly nickname of 'The Three Bears'. Awwwwww!

51

Laxey Partners had been around practically from the birth of Neo-Gers; so why were they selling up now? The Chairman of Laxey, Colin Kingsnorth, explained. Partly it was a bit of a huff over Norman Crighton, who had represented Laxey on the Neo-Gers board, but mostly it was 'in order to halt Ashley's Ibrox takeover.'[22]

The Three Bears now owned 19.5 percent of Neo-Gers. It looked like the Real Rangers Men were gearing up for a fight. 2015 was going to be interesting!

7
Did You No Wrong

January 2015 was a busy time for Neo-Gers. We were barely into the new year when the news emerged that Dave King had bought nearly 15 percent of the club from institutional investors.[1] It looked like those institutional investors wanted out; and yet, the board was expecting other such investors to come flocking to another share issue. Things were beginning to look bleak for the current incumbents of the Blue Room.

King and The Three Bears now owned over thirty percent of Neo-Gers between them; they were at pains to point out, however, that they were not acting in concert. This was due to a little thing called the Takeover Panel.[2] One of the rules concerning companies listed on the Stock Exchange is that anyone buying more than 29.9 percent of the shares is obliged to make an offer for the rest of the company.[3] It might sound crazy, but them's the rules!

And there's more, as Jimmy Cricket used to say. If the other shareholders rebuff the offer for their shares then the individual, or group, which owns more than 29.9% is obliged to sell off their extra shares to bring them back down to the threshold.[4] No wonder King and The Three Bears were so desperate to stress that they were not acting together!

Most folk were convinced that King and the rest *were* acting in concert and one shareholder at Neo-Gers complained to the Takeover Panel. For good measure, the shareholder contacted the Financial Conduct Authority as well.[5]

Of course, some of The People were extremely excited about King and the Three Bears buying shares. A spokesman for Rangers First, one of the groups supporting 'The Real Rangers Men', said:

> This (an upsurge in membership of Rangers First) has
> coincided with a number of well-known Rangers fans also

stepping up with multi-million pound purchases, all of which are a welcome sign of fans "stepping up and playing".[6]

Oh dear! There they went with that hyperbole again! The Three Bears had paid £2.7m for their shares and King wouldn't have paid much more, relatively speaking; hardly what you would call 'multi-million pound purchases'. Still, we should perhaps cut them some slack since they probably couldn't think straight in all the excitement of Real Rangers Men actually buying shares. And, it seemed, not a moment too soon!

There was much wailing and gnashing of teeth when the news emerged that Lewis Macleod had gone to Brentford for the comparatively paltry sum of £850,000! And that wasn't the worst of it. Macleod had actually not wanted to leave and had expected Neo-Gers to fight to hold onto him or, at least, sell him to the highest bidder. Everton and Burnley, both Premiership teams, had expressed an interest and probably would have paid a good deal more. 'Interest', however, wouldn't pay the bills so the Neo-Gers board jumped at the first serious bid to come along. That seriously pissed off Macleod and convinced him that it was time to go.[7]

This desperation for cash flew directly in the face of McMurdo's, and others', contention that Mike Ashley was going to make Neo-Gers into a force to be reckoned with. So far he had invested not a penny; instead he had been drip-feeding loans to the club, keeping it barely alive. Anyone that still thought Ashley was even remotely interested in throwing money at the Ibrox club was seriously deluded.

It had been discovered, back at the start of December, that the Neo-Gers retail contracts only really benefited one party; and it wasn't Neo-Gers! In what seemed a grotesque parody of David Murray's famous saying, for every tenner The People spent on Neo-Gers products the club only got 75p![8] To anyone looking in it was obvious that Ashley was out to make money from Neo-Gers, not put his own money into it.

And so The People were faced with the prospect of their club being run by either a billionaire that was only interested in Number One or a millionaire that also happened to be a convicted criminal. It was hardly a great choice but each side still desperately tried to convince themselves that we were all terrified at the idea of their respective leader being in charge. We could all see, however, that they were doomed no matter which side won.

And then, seemingly out of the blue, somebody else came on the scene that offered an alternative. Perhaps The People might not be faced with a dilemma after all.

Robert Sarver, a billionaire (what else!), turned up on 6th January with an offer to buy the club. Of course, this got some of The People excited, while others were more wary, fearing that Sarver was tied-in with Ashley, Green or even, God forbid, Craig Whyte.

Sarver had to go to the press and reassure them all that he was acting on his own. A spokesman for Sarver said:

> To be very clear, Mr. Sarver has never met or spoken to Mike Ashley, Sandy Easdale or James Easdale. And, for the complete avoidance of doubt, he has never met or spoken to Charles Green or Craig Whyte.[9]

Whoever he was or wasn't connected to, Sarver couldn't have picked a worse time to attempt his takeover bid. King and his cronies had only just bought their shares, so they were hardly going to just give up their fight for power to some Johnny-come-lately. Ashley, too had been fighting off all-comers for months and wasn't going to hand over his cash cow to some other billionaire.

Remember that other rich American that tried to buy Rangers while they were in administration, Bill Miller? He had planned some elaborate shell game, hiding the assets and shuffling things about. Sarver's plans seemed to be needlessly complicated as well. His spokesman outlined what they were:

> The revised proposal involves investing up to £20m for a majority shareholding by way of a placing of new ordinary shares in Rangers at 20 pence per share ('Placing') followed, if the Placing is completed, by a mandatory offer for the remaining issued and to be issued ordinary share capital under Rule 9 of the City Code on Takeovers and Mergers ('Code') at 20 pence per share.
> As part of the revised proposal £6.5m would be made available to Rangers in immediate short-term funding by

way of a secured loan to be repaid in 90 days or out of the proceeds of the Placing.[10]

Well, that certainly cleared things up, eh? With all that stuff about secured loans and repayments from share issues, his proposal hardly looked much different to the situation Neo-Gers was already in. It was just going to be another case of loans followed by more loans. As excitable supporters tend to forget, these guys don't get to be billionaires by being kind-hearted and full of love for their fellow man!

There was also another little matter; what the hell did he want? It was former Rangers chairman, Alastair 'Noddy' Johnston, who brought up this vital question. He said:

> I can't for the life of me understand what his agenda is. There is no obvious connection between him and Rangers, Scotland or football. As far as I'm aware he has no granny in the Highlands.
> I don't think he woke up one morning and said, 'I want to buy a Scottish football team'. Someone must have planted the idea in his mind and it would be better if he told us who that was.[11]

Not surprisingly, Sarver's proposal was thrown out. Hardly anyone mourned when he pulled out altogether. He had had nobody rooting for him among the support or in the media so he'd been on a hiding to nothing right from the start. From looking like being a major player he had gone to being merely another footnote in the Neo-Gers story. Unless, of course, he was to return in the future; stranger things have happened, especially when it comes to Neo-Gers!

Meanwhile, it was Sandy Easdale to the rescue again. It seemed that Neo-Gers had defaulted on national insurance payments (that sounded familiar) and HMRC had issued them with a 'seven-day notice letter' at the end of December 2014. Big Sandy had to stump up a loan of £500,000 to stop the club being wound up.[12] He would be repaid once the money for the sale of Lewis Macleod arrived.

So there was another thing for The People to get riled about; the relative pittance that Macleod had been sold for was merely to pay for a short-term fix. That was why the Neo-Gers board had been

56

unwilling, indeed, unable, to await a possible higher bid for Macleod. They needed the money quickly so had to just accept whatever they could get. It was hardly what anyone could call a great business plan.

And the bad news just kept on coming. The SFA decided to reject the Neo-Gers appeal and uphold the SPFL's ruling that the new club had to stump up the £250,000 fine imposed by Lord Nimmo-Smith.[13] There was no way the cash-strapped club could afford this, unless, of course, it sold more of its squad. Unfortunately, there were no other players left that any other club would want. Perhaps some two-for-one deal involving Boyd and Miller might raise a few bob... As it turned out, the Neo-Gers board decided to defer the problem by demanding that it be taken to arbitration.

The 16th of January added to the farce, as well as highlighting the cash crisis at Neo-Gers. It was one of those silly Friday-night matches that are being forced upon punters by television companies. Neo-Gers versus Hearts; a huge game in terms of determining the top spot, which Hearts looked like running away with. As the snow fell, and folk struggled to make their way into Glasgow, radios were listened to intently in case the match was called off. It wasn't.

Like most stadia, Ibrox is equipped with undersoil heating, meaning that a bit of snow needn't stop a match. Unfortunately, nobody at Ibrox had a shilling for the meter so the undersoil heating remained switched to OFF. The players came on for a practice kick about and promptly skidded everywhere and fell on their arses. Inexplicably, Bobby Madden, the referee decided to go ahead.

Also inexplicably, a yellow ball was used instead of an orange one. This wasn't one of your Nike Hi-Vis balls[14] either; it was just a yellow Mitre. In fact, the players' boots were more visible than the ball![15] Fortunately, there were no patches of yellow snow on the pitch to test the ball's visibility even further!

The match lasted all of twenty-five minutes before Madden decided that enough was enough and blew the whistle to end the farce. Understandably, the spectators were not too happy with the situation and stewards had to stop fights breaking out between rival sets of supporters.[16] The whole thing was a travesty and everyone had to trudge out of the stadium to make their way home in the snow.

Meanwhile, the smeggy-bedsheet brigade was outside demonstrating, as was their wont at any Neo-Gers home match.

(More about that later.) Hearts fans leaving the stadium had to run a gauntlet of The People, spitting, throwing objects and smashing the windows of supporters' buses.[17] As if things weren't bad enough having to make their way back along the M8, in dangerous conditions, after a complete waste of a journey to Glasgow!

To make things even more farcical, Kenny McDowall, who had taken over as interim manager when Ally went off to mow a few lawns, decided, just a couple of days later, to hand in his notice. Just like Ally had promised, McDowall was going to stay until his twelve-month notice was up. He cited 'personal reasons' for his decision to quit. A simple Neo-Gers statement said,

> Kenny, who has been a fantastic servant of the club, will serve his 12-month notice period, during which time he will remain 100 per cent committed to his normal duties. The club respects Kenny's decision and he will continue to have the full support of everybody at Rangers.[18]

He would also continue to pocket a healthy wage packet at Neo-Gers' expense!

The Real Rangers Men and their supporters, in the meantime, were up in arms. On January 13th 'Notices of Security' were lodged with the Register of Scotland. These notices are what is required in order to stop anyone using a particular property or piece of land as security for a loan. This is normally done when the person that lodged the notices is intending to use the land or property as collateral himself. These particular 'Notices of Security' concerned Ibrox Park and Murray Park.

Neo-Gers needed money and it looked like Ashley was ready to line up another loan; the figure being bandied about was £10m. Unfortunately, it also looked as if he was demanding Ibrox Park and Murray Park as collateral.[19] The People were outraged to say the least. That's why they were demonstrating with the pish-stained bedsheets outside Ibrox on the 16th.

In the chaos after the match was abandoned some of the demonstrators decided to take the opportunity to take their protest to another level. There were reports of stadium offices being broken into[20] and worse; much worse. Other stories began to emerge of workers being attacked; specifically, a woman and an eighty-year-old man.[21] While McMurdo and his followers denounced this violence, they were strangely mute about the attacks on the Hearts supporters.

One of the contributors to McMurdo's blog was concerned about the media picking up the story:

> If this is true then you have probably given some lazy arse journalist a story. Otherwise if they had even a sniff of this it would be all over the news and papers magnified, perhaps in tomorrows papers. They will have a field day and more.[22]

Obviously they still didn't quite understand what the agenda of the Scottish media was; they were even now using phrases like 'Rangers-hating' media. What the agenda really was became all too clear when the media pretty much ignored the story of the assaults. The perpetrators were supporters of the Real Rangers Men, after all; just like the Scottish media.

And so we had, on the one hand, the Scottish media being quite content to report about the violence against the Hearts supporters. This section of The People was fair game; as paying customers they were evidently supporting the current board. On the other hand, McMurdo and his cronies were happy to condemn the violence perpetrated by the anti-board faction. Our Fourth Estate, at the same time, ignored the violence of the bedsheet wavers, while the McMurdo side turned a blind eye to the assaults carried out by the ordinary supporters. This was going beyond a mere internecine struggle; it was becoming a full-scale civil war.

The Commander-in-Chief of the bedsheet wavers, Dave King, carried out a more practical manoeuvre on that evening of the 16th January. He demanded that an Emergency General Meeting be called, which he was perfectly entitled to do as the biggest shareholder. The board was going to have to acquiesce to his demand; they could prevaricate, of course, but they would eventually have to hold an EGM. King was confident now that he had enough backing and that the Real Rangers Men would win the day.[23]

Of course, good PR is always important in these circumstances. Although Jack Irvine was not officially connected to Ibrox any more, he did work for the Easdale family, which entitled him to still speak out on matters Neo-Gers. Before January was out he was straight in there, reminding everyone that Dave King and Paul Murray were on the board that sold Rangers to Craig Whyte for a pound.[24] King and Co. were going to need to engage their own PR, and fast.

Luckily there was a new player in town. On 13th January a company, calling itself Level 5 PR, launched in what it claimed to be 'state of the art offices' in Blythswood Square in Glasgow. It was rather an unfortunate address for a PR firm to choose. The elegant buildings of Blythswood Square are home to many respectable and prestigious companies, organisations and professions. The area, however, is forever indelibly linked with only one particular profession; the oldest one.

Level 5 PR has only two directors listed, a Mr. Stephen Kerr and a Mr. James Sexton Traynor.[25] That's right; our old pal Jabba was now running his own PR firm! Considering the way Traynor insulted every journalist in the land in his last article for the Daily Record, and the way he threatened everyone in the Fourth Estate with litigation while he was working at Neo-Gers, it was debatable how effective he was going to be as a PR representative. As it turned out, however, that wasn't going to be a major problem.

The official website for Level 5 PR tells us that Traynor was Director of Communications at Rangers (sic). Stephen Kerr, we are informed, was Press Officer at Rangers for nine years.[26] Among those providing testimonials are Walter Smith and Roddy Forsyth, a well-known cheerleader for the Ibrox club.[27] Can you detect a pattern emerging here?

In among a description of the services they offer, Level 5 PR includes what could be construed as a sort of mission statement: 'We offer a specialised, personal service based on trust, morality, belief and integrity and we take on only those clients who share our core values and ideals.'[28] Oh dear! That'll explain why one of their first clients was a convicted criminal, then!

Of course, you can't have Jabba around without some inadvertent comedy being present as well. Walter Smith provided the punchlines. 'The one thing you will always get from James Traynor is honesty,' he said.[29] Er…so was he being honest when he said that Rangers was dead in the Daily Record or when, a short time later, he insisted that the club he was now working for was 'still Rangers'?

Smith continues: 'He is a listener and I also found through the years that he has a way of solving all kinds of problems through logic and reason.'[30] Really? I don't remember much listening being done on his Radio Scotland phone-in show, where he had a tendency to shout folk down. And if he didn't agree with somebody his solution was usually to insult them and then cut them off; he always did it in a logical and reasonable way, though!

When it became clear that Traynor's company was representing the Real Rangers Men, all was forgiven. Despite having been bad-mouthed by Jabba, the esteemed members of our media fell over themselves to report every soundbite offered by Level 5 PR. Every picture accompanying the latest utterances from King and his cronies had the name Level 5 prominently displayed in the background. It was like the good old days; this time, though, the handouts were coming *from* Traynor instead of *to* him.

On an amusing side note, all the pictures of King, and the rest of the Real Rangers Men, spouting pish at the Level 5 offices, were available to buy from SNS group.[31] You could buy the pictures in a variety of formats; framed, canvas print, photographic print or as wallpaper for your computer. The pictures were priced from £2.99 to £59.99; so there was something to suit every pocket. 'The Perfect Gift' the website announced; I wonder who'd thank you for a gift like that! The prints are still available to buy, so form an orderly queue!

As well as the return of Jabba, another character appeared for an encore. To The People, however, this other reappearance was about as welcome as a fart in a confessional box. It was good old Charlie Green, he of the big hands and French chateau; back to get the sphincters of the Neo-Gers supporters all a-quiver.

We'd heard about Green before this, of course; a horse of his, called 'Ibrox', ran in a race in France and came in eighth.[32] Green himself told the Daily Record, 'The colours are red, white and blue — be in no doubt. I called the horse Ibrox to keep the memory of Rangers in my mind. They are close to my heart.'[33]

Charlie was obviously of the impression that The People were easily gulled, while the Daily Record seemed to have the same, low opinion of the rest of us. In this day-and-age it's a simple matter to look things up on the internet; a quick search revealed that the jockey astride the brute was actually clad in silks of green and pink. Charlie was evidently still fond of taking the piss![34]

Such appearances of Chateau Charlie in the press might amuse the rest of us but, to The People, they were like a stake through the heart. Charlie's puss was a constant reminder that the Big Lie was just that; a lie. If he could just be airbrushed from the history of Ibrox then it would be easier to pretend that it was still the same club; still Rangers. Every time Charlie popped up in the media we were all reminded of words like 'liquidation', 'assets' and 'Sevco'. No wonder The People got so upset!

January 2015, however, seemed to bring good news at last. A rumour began to do the rounds on the internet that Charles Green had been arrested in France.[35] Quite why he should have been arrested is a complete mystery. Apparently, The People thought that if they took a dislike to someone then the UK police forces, Interpol and the Sûreté should be straight on the case.

The excitement, however, turned out to be premature; Charlie was actually in a London hospital, having an operation on his knee![36] A picture of said knee, suitably bandaged, appeared everywhere to prove the point. The injured limb was probably viewed more times on the internet than Kim Kardashian's arse.

The poor, old bugger had scarcely come round from the anaesthetic when he was confronted by Jim White, ready to do an interview, in his usual shouty manner, for Sky Sports.[37] Green got angry and even tearful as he argued his case. He didn't take anything more than he was entitled to; in fact, he took less. His salary, apparently, was halved, while Sooperally clung doggedly to his massive wage packet. To the relief of many of The People, he reiterated the Big Lie, insisting that 'Rangers' had been cast out of the SPL into the lower leagues. To their dismay, however, he hinted at a possible return to Ibrox. He also suggested that they all got behind Ashley and the board.

The Daily Record was quick to point out the discrepancies in Green's argument. Although he claimed to have been on £360,000 a year, he actually raked in £933,000 for ten months at Ibrox;[38] a good deal more than Sooperally! The Record, who supported the Real Rangers Men with a vengeance, was at pains to point out that Green was as mad as a hatter. They even had a poll, asking if the hospital interview was 'the most bonkers thing you've ever seen'.[39]

While the Daily Record was laughing at Green and cheering on the Real Rangers Men, the paper's hero, Dave King, was not having it all his own way. Yes, an EGM was going to have to be called but the month ended with the Neo-Gers board accepting another loan from Ashley. This time it was for ten million quid. It wasn't going to be available all in a 'wanner', but in two separate tranches of £5m. The first tranche was drawn down almost immediately; as usual, Neo-Gers was skint.

Unfortunately, the £5m wasn't going to last very long, since £3m of it was being used to pay off Ashley's previous loans. The money also came, as it always seemed to do at Ibrox, with conditions attached. Sports Direct got another chunk of Neo-Gers's retail, taking it up to a 75% share, while all shirt sponsorship revenue would be handed over to 'Rangers Retail Limited' from the 2017-2018 season until the loan was paid off.[40]

At the rate Neo-Gers went through cash, paying for Sooperally's grass seeds and daffodil bulbs, it wouldn't take too long before the second £5m would have to be drawn down. That's when things were going to get serious. Before the board could get its grubby, collective hands on this second tranche, they would have to wait until Sports Direct carried out due diligence. That would no doubt mean new agreements and new onerous contracts.[41]

There was also a time limit on repayment of the second tranche; five years from the date it was drawn down. It was normal for Neo-Gers to have to scrape together the cash just to pay the monthly wage bill; raking in the bins for ginger bottles and taking bits of the stadium down to the scrappie. How the hell was such a cash-starved entity as Neo-Gers going to find £5m; even if they had five years to do it? It's not as if they can sell more signed photos or bits of grass from the pitch; that would have to be done through 'Rangers Retail Limited'! The only recourse would be more loans and, with no bank to go to, Ashley would be the sole option.

The only way to escape Ashley's onerous contracts would be through administration; but even then Ashley had things sewn up.
Sports Direct had a floating charge over Murray Park, Edmiston House, the Albion Car Park and even the club's trademarks. This meant that they would be allowed to appoint the administrator if the club defaulted on repaying the loan.[42]

Of course, this got the bedsheet wavers all in a fluster and the consensus among them and the media was that the Real Rangers Men couldn't take over quickly enough. Before that happened,
though, there was a little matter that would manage to unite The Peeppul; for a while, at any rate. There was a match taking place in February that the media were building up to the heavens.

8
Silly Thing

'**I**t's the Big One!' That's what Ian Crocker used to say on Sky Sports whenever he was introducing an Old Firm match. And this is the way that our media had been building up the League Cup semi-final between Celtic and Neo-Gers ever since the draw had been made at the end of October. The Daily Record, of course, was right in the van of promoting this as the first Old Firm match in years.

'THE first Old Firm clash since April 2012' and 'They'll meet Ronny Deila's men at Hampden for the first time in two and a half years,' the Record claimed.[1] The Big Lie, of course, was given an airing. 'Rangers...will play the Hoops for the first time since their *demotion* to the Third Division'[2] (My italics) and 'Rangers' priority is still to earn promotion *back* to the top flight'[3] (My italics) reinforced the story that this was the latest in a long line of Old Firm derbies. And these quotes are all from the same article!

Many people predicted trouble at the match and the media concurred, with their usual two-faced moral indignation while slavering at the prospect. The police, however, seemed ready to clamp down on trouble of any kind. Police officers were taught the lyrics to banned songs, so that they could recognise them and make appropriate arrests.[4] (Some wags suggested it was so they could join in!) The police even visited known perpetrators of domestic violence to forestall any instances of wife-beating.[5] It looked like our boys in blue were definitely on the case.

The People, as was their wont, believed that the police were only interested in the singing of Celtic supporters. Bill McMurdo said, 'Apparently Scotland's Finest must distinguish between illegal songs glorifying terrorist murderers and legal songs glorifying terrorist murderers. Yes, it is that stoopid.'[6] No mention, of course, of The People's songbook of hatred for Catholics and the Irish!

A week before the match was to take place, a group of Celtic supporters took out a full-page advert in the Sunday Herald, pointing out the mendacity of the Big Lie and that this would be the first meeting of Celtic and the new club based at Ibrox.[7] Of course, this had The People, and everyone with any connection to Ibrox, foaming at the mouth.

Ex-Ranger Bert Konterman said:

> I have seen the same in Holland at PEC Zwolle, the team I joined as a young lad. When I came in, it was PEC Zwolle, it was FC Zwolle when I played there and the name went back to PEC. The shirt changed a little bit as well, but, overall, it is the same club. It is the same stadium, it is the same history.[8]

That sounded like the same desperate argument that The People grabbed onto when Rangers was first liquidated; all the 'Pacific Shelf' nonsense. Unfortunately for them, however, the argument is completely flawed and means nothing.

At the end of the Nineteenth Century there was an area of West-Central Africa called French Congo. This subsequently became Middle Congo, Republic of the Congo, the People's Republic of the Congo and then back to the Republic of the Congo. Despite all these name changes, flag changes and regime changes the area remained the same country with the same population.

By way of contrast, whenever anyone spoke of 'Russia' in the 1970s and 1980s, they were referring to the USSR, the Union of Soviet Socialist Republics. After the fall of Communism, the USSR dissolved into a number of separate states, including the Russian Federation. Nowadays, 'Russia' means the Russian Federation and nothing else; in fact, Estonians, Lithuanians and citizens of all the other nations that used to be in the USSR take great umbrage at being called 'Russian'.

'Russia', then, means two different things depending on when it was said. In old movies and books, it means the Soviet Union; in today's newspapers it refers to the Russian Federation. It's the same name but two entirely different entities.

Like the Republic of the Congo, and PEC Zwolle for that matter, a club can be called The Celtic Football and Athletic Company Limited, Pacific Shelf 595 Limited, Celtic Football Club PLC or any other name you can come up with but the fact remains that it is, and always has been, the same team. Like the Soviet Union, or Russia, Rangers was liquidated and disappeared from existence. And, just like Russia, you can call the new club at Ibrox 'Rangers' all you like; it doesn't make it the same entity.

One of the regular commenters on McMurdo's blog pointed to a supposedly-neutral observer, who ridiculed the advert in the Sunday Herald.[9] Far from being neutral, however, this character constantly spouts hatred for Manchester United and, by extension, for Celtic, whose fans, he claims, all support United as their 'second team'. It was hardly a disinterested opinion!

One point this character, Rob Atkinson, had to make was interesting. He said:

> So what is the one thread that runs right through a club's very soul and being? It is the fans, the loyal supporters who follow, follow, through thick and thin, passing on the supporting tradition down the generations.[10]

Let's pursue that line of thinking for a moment. Let's assume that the only important thing is the fans; what happens to the club is irrelevant. Okay? Now have a wee read of what another blogger, Photobhoy, has discovered about a team called Eastern Rovers.[11] For those with no access to the internet (or who can't be bothered!), here is a quick summary of what Photobhoy has to tell us.

He discovered an article in the Glasgow Observer, dated 11th July 1885, which tells us that:

> A meeting was held on Thursday of the young men of the Sacred Heart Parish for the purpose of reorganising the old football club of the parish…After some discussion it was resolved to adhere to the old name of the Eastern Rovers, which had been raised though the exertions of Brother Walfrid.

Photobhoy wonders if this team was a precursor to Celtic but, taking Rob Atkinson's line, with which a lot of The People no doubt agree, it could possibly be a lot more than that. It could well be that those that went along to cheer on Eastern Rovers later went to Celtic Park. And you will notice that Eastern Rovers was not a new club in 1885; the meeting was 'for the purpose of reorganising the old football club'. You've probably already guessed what I'm driving at here.

If the same fans supported Celtic that previously supported Eastern Rovers, then it could be argued that Celtic was actually a *continuation* of Eastern Rovers. The involvement of Brother Walfrid in both certainly helps this argument. Since Eastern Rovers was being 'reorganised' in 1885 and is described in that year as 'the old football club', one wonders when the club was initially formed. Could it be that Celtic, previously called Eastern Rovers, was founded before those 'Gallant Pioneers' met up in 1872?

Oh dear! The People certainly wouldn't like that! But if they're going to argue that all that matters is 'the fans' then they can't start complaining if the argument leads to conclusions they don't like!

Anyway, the Sunday Herald advert riled up The People immeasurably. Those that wrote it were variously called delusional, trouble makers, wrong-headed, Rangers-Haters and, incredibly, bigots. The best one, though, came from ex-Rangers player Alex Rae. While questioning the conduct of those that wrote the advert, he said, 'Rangers, over the years, have tried to conduct themselves in the right manner, with a bit of dignity.'[12] Tell that to the people of Manchester or to all those that were shafted when liquidation occurred. Rae himself was always a bit of a thug as a player; even kicking into an opponent's head while he was on the ground.[13] He always lashed out with dignity, though!

The way everything had been built up a bloodbath was expected, with our media anticipating off-the-radar violence with ghoulish relish. In this respect, the match turned out to be a complete anti-climax. There were no missiles flying about and no pitched battles in the street. The only thing that happened was that a boy was hit by a flying bottle and lost a couple of teeth; and by God, wasn't a meal made of that incident!

The story was that a bus, carrying Neo-Gers supporters, was attacked by a crowd of Celtic fans. No windows were broken or anything; it seems that it was all just words and gestures. That was until somebody opened the door. We've never heard who it was that opened the door; did somebody outside use the emergency handle, or did somebody on the bus want to go outside for a square go? Whatever the truth a bottle was thrown onto the bus and the boy got hit in the face.

Over the next few days the boy and his brother attended Lennoxtown training ground as Celtic did its bit to make it up to the lad.[14] In pictures of the visit the two boys didn't exactly look too chuffed to be there![15] A few days later, the boys were mascots, leading out the team at Ibrox. One commenter in the Herald had this to say:

It was good to see this young child and his brother out on the pitch yesterday enjoying themselves being mascots at the team

67

they actually support and smiling.....
It will no doubt take a long time for these children to get over the
trauma they have both suffered going to a football match because
of sectarian supporting fans of Celtic.[16]

This particular individual must have been looking at the wrong boys,
since pictures of the event prove that the lads were just as miserable-
looking as they had been at Lennoxtown.[17] It certainly looks as if the
boys are not that interested in football and probably had to be dragged
out the house to go to Hampden in the first place!

The incident showed a remarkable difference in the reactions of Celtic
supporters and The People. A Celtic fan started up an online collection
and raised thousands from other Celtic supporters, who expressed their
shame that one of their fellows could be responsible for such a thing.[18]
The People, on the other hand, were less concerned about the boy and
more keen on vengeance. A businessman offered £1000 for information
leading to an arrest. Another businessman then doubled that offer and
claimed he would keep doubling it until somebody came forward.[19]
There has been no reply to this offer as yet; perhaps they're waiting until
it reaches a million!

The real reason, of course, why the media was concentrating so much
on this incident was to deflect from the disgraceful singing at the match
itself. All the old favourites were given an airing, including 'The Billy
Boys' and 'The Famine Song'. Somebody claimed to have strained his
ears and heard 'IRA' being shouted, but it might well have been the guy
on the PA, struggling to compete with 'No Pope of Rome' as he
explained where the fire exits were.

Of course, our media couldn't report such a thing without the need to
'balance things out'. As if the singing coming from The People wasn't
bad enough, those evil bounders in the Green Brigade held up a banner
with the word 'Huns' on it![20]

There's no point in going into the desperate attempts to make out that
the word 'Huns' is sectarian. Suffice it to say that the supporters of just
about every team in Scotland are not averse to singing, 'Go home ya
Huns!' Does that make all those people anti-Protestant? As for the
argument about how the word is used in Northern Ireland, there's a
perfectly simple counter-argument; this isn't Northern Ireland. Flag
down a black cab and you'll get it to yourself!

It's hardly surprising that nothing ever gets done about sectarian

68

bigotry in Scotland when nobody is willing to tackle it without trying to blame the victims as well as the perpetrators. We'll come back to this disgraceful 'whatabootery' later.

As usual, the conclusion of the SPFL was that Neo-Gers had no case to answer. It was the old argument of the club 'doing all it could' to eradicate bigotry and so it could not be punished. Rather generously, they decided that Celtic had no case to answer either![21]

In among all this carry-on there was actually a football match happened. Unfortunately, the match turned out to be a bit of a disappointment. Celtic supporters had been predicting a score reflective of a rugby match, but the game ended in a mere two-nil victory. Meanwhile, Neo-Gers were shown up as being a lot poorer than the Premiership-ready team they had been claiming to be. Craig Gordon finished the match not only with a clean sheet but with clean gloves as well!

It's probable that folk in the rest of the world watching the match missed the two goals and didn't even notice the vile sing-song; they were too busy laughing at what passes as a national stadium in Scotland. The pitch was an absolute disgrace and looked more like Paschendale (or Passchendaele, as it seems to be called nowadays) than a football field. The SFA couldn't even blame the previous day's semi-final for the state of the pitch; it had been just as bad when Dundee United and Aberdeen were playing. Perhaps they wanted to show how skint Scottish football was due to there being no Rangers in the top tier; that 'Armageddon' they'd been predicting.

There were dark murmurs that the pitch was deliberately in that state to stop Celtic's style of play, but it didn't help Neo-Gers either. Hopeful punts up the field are all very well but somebody needs to be there to receive the delivery. Kenny Miller tried and nearly broke his leg in one of the many potholes. He was, however, awarded a free kick for his troubles!

Kenny Miller, rather laughably, suggested that the match showed that there was not much of a gulf between the two teams,[22] but he was kidding nobody but himself. He pointed to the second-half performance of Neo-Gers but, in reality, Celtic were being extremely careful in the second half. The game was already won and Neo-Gers weren't posing much of a threat; so why should Celtic risk injuries on that surface? Miller seems not to have noticed but, despite the great 'performance' he spoke of, Neo-Gers didn't even manage one shot on target.

Miller's team-mate, Richard Foster, was more realistic in his assessment: 'We've watched videos of them at Parkhead and they do move the ball quickly. But with the pitch being like it was, it might have slowed them down a little bit and helped us.'[23]

It certainly looked as if a lot more work needed to be done if Neo-Gers wanted to be playing week-in, week-out in the Big Boys' league!

9
Bodies

'**R**angers will finish in the top two now and will be good
enough to go through the play-offs, that's a guarantee. I
believe with these five players Rangers will only go from
strength to strength.'[1]

Thus spake Olivier Bernard, former Rangers and Newcastle United
player. He was commenting on the news that, in the closing hours of
the transfer window, a job-lot of five players was being sent up on
loan from Newcastle to Neo-Gers. It looked like the association with
Mike Ashley was finally paying off!

Of course, not everyone was happy about this development, least
of all Hearts and Hibs! There was nothing, however, that anybody
could do about it since there were no laws to stop multiple, cross-
border loans. There was even a precedent with all those loan moves
years ago from FC Kaunas to Hearts. Other teams could moan all
they liked; they would just have to put up with it.

Gael Bigirimana, Shane Ferguson, Kevin Mbabu, Remie Streete
and Haris Vuckic were all fringe players at Newcastle United; but
even an EPL fringe player is normally beyond the finances of teams
in Scotland. It was reckoned that this move would be viewed as
further proof of Ashley's undue influence at Ibrox when he was up
before the SFA on March 2nd.[2] That was certainly the hope of Chris
'Ze List' Graham and the rest of the Real Rangers Men supporters.

It was only a week after the match against Celtic that Neo-Gers
were in cup action again. It was the Scottish Cup fifth round against
their old nemesis, Raith Rovers. This time, though, it was going to be
different. As Kenny Miller had said, there was not much to choose
between Neo-Gers and Celtic. And then there were those five high-
flyers from Newcastle. It was going to be a walkover.

The People, however, didn't quite see it that way. Less than eleven-
and-a-half thousand turned up to the match, even though it was at
Ibrox. Many of those, moreover, were only there to shout at the folk
in the Directors' Box. Mind you, that was probably a lot more

entertaining than watching the crap served up by their team on the pitch! Yes, it was another defeat as Kenny McDowall continued Sooperally's record of failing in every cup competition Neo-Gers took part in.

2-1 was the final score and even five minutes added on couldn't help Neo-Gers as Raith looked the more likely to hit the back of the net even then.[3] Neo-Gers did their usual huffing and puffing; having most of the possession but doing nothing with it. It was obvious that the previous week's score at Hampden had flattered Neo-Gers immensely.

The only bright spot in the whole match, as far as The People were concerned, was that Haris Vuckic appeared to be a lot better than anybody else playing at Ibrox. It looked like the loans from NUFC might be a great deal after all. Rather ominously, however, another of the five, Remie Streete, limped off before half-time and had to be replaced.

The team were roundly booed and verbally abused as they went off at full-time. The abuse was all the more vitriolic given the fact that there was nobody in the Directors' Box to hear the demonstrations against the board; the board members had been warned by the police not to attend.[4] McDowall and his team, therefore, had to bear the full brunt of The People's anger. And, by God, weren't The People angry!

The Real Rangers Men faction had picked up on Bomber Brown's use of the word 'rats' and said rodent had now become a common motif on all the painted bedsheets. Every banner had a rat on it, like an early Stranglers album; even the banner unfurled to cheers inside the ground had a couple of rats on it, with pound signs in their eyes.[5]

It was rather unfortunate that most of the banners manufactured by The People tended to show a distinct lack of originality, as well as a distinct lack of wit. If a similar situation were to arise at Celtic, you can be sure that the Green Brigade, and others, would be brandishing banners that would make everyone laugh as well as getting the point across. I can imagine something along the lines of Peggy Mitchell, clad in a Celtic top, yelling, 'Gerrourra my club!' The People seem never to have mastered the art of humour.

Then again, perhaps the red mist had descended so far that none of them was able to concentrate on anything either original or humorous! They had their EGM to look forward to but the board was doing its best to make sure that very few of them would be able to attend.

It was not altogether surprising when the Neo-Gers board decided to book a London hotel to hold the EGM. After the disgraceful scenes at the AGM and the assault on Ibrox staff during the Hearts match, you could hardly blame the board members for wanting to avoid any trouble. As we've already noted, they had even been warned by the police that it was too dangerous for them to attend a match at their own stadium!

The Real Rangers Men mob, however, were outraged. The hotel in question, the Millennium Gloucester, could only hold 500,[6] so, even if The People were to travel down to London, there was no way they would be allowed in. the papers were full of angry quotes from the Union of Vanguard First Sons of Struth Trust or whatever they called themselves.

By February 9th another venue was being sought. The Neo-Gers board explained what had happened.

> The hotel management at the Millennium Gloucester has taken advice from different quarters and concluded that the GM cannot be managed without significant disruption to guests and neighbours. The hotel management felt it necessary to take this position after receiving numerous complaints and false information from individuals purporting to be shareholders.[7]

No doubt some of The People's trademark death threats were involved as well.

Another venue was booked, the Grange Tower Bridge Hotel, which, just like the first venue, cancelled almost as soon as it was announced. The Daily Record reported a hotel spokesperson saying, 'There is no question when it comes to the comfort and security of our guests and staff. We do not compromise on this.'[8] The paper also quoted one of the Real Rangers Men in a desperate attempt to blame Celtic supporters for the cancellation.[9]

Roddy Forsyth, in the Telegraph, admitted that the hotel had actually received threats but, again, the blame seemed to be put onto Celtic supporters.[10] Quite why Celtic supporters should do this, when they were anticipating The People being rounded up by the

Metropolitan Police and sent 'homewards tae think again', was never explained. Perhaps Chelsea supporters were getting fed up of taking the blame! Anyway, there was only one mob that benefited from these hotels canceling and said mob had already been employing intimidation, verbal abuse and even physical assault to try to get its own way.

So now the EGM was going to be held at Ibrox, as the Real Rangers Men and their followers had wanted all along. The date was also put back to the 6th March, giving the Sons of the Union of Struth First more time to practise drawing rats. It also gave added time for the war of words in the media.

At the end of January Paul Murray had this to say:

> In the lead up to the General Meeting the usual suspects will attempt to undermine our cause because they realise their days could be numbered. The truth is that for the first time in years there is a group of people capable of rebuilding and repairing our club and malicious speculation will not deflect us.[11]

Of course, the board released a statement about the Real Rangers Men at the same time as their initial announcement regarding the EGM.[12] Malicious? Most certainly? Speculation? That was debatable. What wasn't debatable was that the statement was correct as far as the fitness of King and Murray went. Both were directors of the old 'company' and were therefore effectively banned from taking seats on the current board. Or, at least, that was the way things were supposed to work.

And then there was Honest Dave himself. A convicted criminal was hardly what you could call a 'fit and proper person' and the board's statement made sure to repeat the South African judge's appraisal of King as a 'mendacious witness' and a 'glib and shameless liar'.[13] The Real Rangers Men might not like it but everything the board's statement said was true.

The real clincher, as far as the board was concerned, was that the current Nominated Adviser (NOMAD), WH Ireland, was intending to resign if the Real Rangers Men took over. This would mean immediate suspension from the AIM stock market and the possibility of Neo-Gers being kicked out permanently if another NOMAD wasn't in place within a month.[14]

While all these off-field shenanigans were happening, matters on the pitch were as bad as ever. On 13th February, after the debacles of the cup games, it was back to league duty. Hibs came to Ibrox, having already beaten Neo-Gers on their last two encounters. This match was to offer up no surprises and Hibs won quite comfortably by 2-0. According to the BBC, Neo-Gers actually put up a reasonable enough showing, though their finishing left a lot to be desired.[15]

Again, Vuckic was the star of the show and delivered excellent balls into the Hibs goal area. Unfortunately, there was nobody else in the team worthy of his talent and his deliveries constantly failed to be converted. Boyd at one stage could only manage to kick out at the ball and end up on his arse![16]

The demonstrators were outside, of course, fired up by the upcoming EGM. The 'rats' motif was really taking hold by now; there were even folk wearing rat masks, giving a pantomime feel to the whole thing. Tam Shepherd's must have been doing a roaring trade! Rather disappointingly, Bomber Brown wasn't wearing a Pied Piper outfit; instead, he sported, appropriately enough, a leather bomber jacket.

Joining Bomber at the demonstration that evening were Iain Ferguson and Nacho Novo.[17] You had to laugh at Novo's participation in these events; if somebody on the board had come out and shoved a contract under his nose, he'd switch sides quicker than one of those rats up a drainpipe! After all, he spent half of 2013 trying to suck up to the Neo-Gers board to see if they'd sign him.[18] Maybe he was hoping to be part of the plans of the Real Rangers Men

10
Belsen Was a Gas

'Please sign my petition asking all sponsors and broadcasters to boycott #RFC games as "Up to our knees in Fenian Blood" isn't acceptable.'[1]

This is what Stan Collymore put on Twitter on 19th February, causing The People to go absolutely berserk. His message didn't go down too well with the Scottish media either. The Daily Record called him a 'controversial pundit' and a 'self-proclaimed anti-fascist' and made sure to point out that at the League Cup semi-final there had been 'an offensive banner in the Hoops end'.[2]

It's something that the Scottish media has always liked to pretend doesn't happen; a bit like when Rangers had a sectarian signing policy. On the rare occasions when it is acknowledged, they always drag Celtic into it, with 'both sides as bad as each other' and 'two sides of the same coin' arguments. It's Scotland's dirty little secret and our media get particularly upset when an outsider highlights it.

Of course, Collymore was subjected to the trademark death threats, as well as aspersions being cast on his abilities as a player. There was also the matter of his punching his then girlfriend, Ulrika Jonsson, a few years back. Apparently, being guilty of such a crime excludes you from having an opinion on anything. And it wasn't just The People that brought this up.

One of the Daily Record's staff, Euan McLean, said:

> …it's a bit rich for a guy to preach from the moral high ground when he has previous for beating up his girlfriend. And starting a petition on Twitter to get Rangers games taken off the telly, followed by comments about censorship and fascism sounded like the rantings of a man losing the plot.[3]

He also spoke of the problem of 'religious bigotry at Ibrox and Parkhead'. There we go with Celtic being dragged into it again.

One of the many Neo-Gers supporters groups, the Rangers Supporters Trust, said, 'If Mr. Collymore was interested in sectarianism then he would deal with the subject evenly.'[4] In other words, 'What aboot theym?'

A word has been coined for this way of thinking: 'whatabootery'. Euan McLean referred to it, saying that 'fans of both Rangers and Celtic are skilled in the art.'[5] And there's where the problem lies, right there. Mr. McLean is indulging in his own bit of 'whatabootery' there. He, like every other member of the Fourth Estate in Scotland, can't just deal with the issue in front of him; he's got to drag Celtic into it as well.

The fact is, despite what our media would have us believe, you actually don't get Celtic supporters indulging in 'whatabootery'. On the contrary, Celtic supporters don't feel the need since they claim that their songs and chants are not sectarian or bigoted. And they have a point. When did anyone last hear Celtic fans singing or chanting about wanting to kill, or even hating, Protestants? The answer most folk will give is: never. There's apparently an 'add-on' to the Soldier Song that says, 'Soon there'll be no Protestants at all,' but I must say, I've never heard it. I've read somewhere that it used to be sung in the 1970s but that was a long time ago.

Probably the most revered individual at Celtic Park, and among Celtic supporters, is not Brother Walfrid, the founder, or Jimmy Johnstone, voted the greatest-ever player; it's Jock Stein, who guided Celtic to nine league titles in a row and to being the first team in the whole of Northern Europe to win the European Cup. He also happens to have been a Protestant. So much for sectarian bigotry at Celtic Park.

That, however, does not stop our media from constantly implying that Celtic supporters are just as bad as The People in the sectarian bigotry stakes. The fact that they have to go to extraordinary lengths to try to prove the case shows what a load of garbage the accusation is.

There's the word 'Hun' for example. We have already noted that the supporters of other teams throughout Scotland use that word to refer to the team from Ibrox and its fans. Even the minority of Hearts supporters that are not averse to a rousing chorus of 'The Billy Boys' will still talk of 'The Huns'. It is not a sectarian term. It has always just referred to Rangers and its supporters and, since

Neo-Gers has the same support, claiming that the team is 'still Rangers', the word 'Huns' has been transferred to the new club along with the SFA licence.

Nacho Novo, Jorg Albertz and Lorenzo Amoruso might be Catholics but they are also Huns, having played for Rangers and still counting themselves among the supporters. So how can the word possibly be viewed as sectarian? That, however, doesn't stop the claims that it is.

Nil By Mouth, for example, the anti-sectarian charity, says that the word is a sectarian, abusive term used against Protestants.[6] They offer not a shred of evidence for this claim; they obviously haven't looked too deeply into the subject of sectarianism. That becomes plain when they also make the ridiculous assertion that 'Tim' is a sectarian term. I don't think I've ever seen that word used with offensive intent; nor perceived as such by those called 'Tims'. They're really clutching at straws there!

Whenever any discussion of sectarian bigotry rears its head the media, and anti-bigotry organisations, always have to preserve what they call 'a balanced view'. Essentially, this means arguing that Celtic supporters and The People are as bad as each other. Sometimes they have to try to create some phantom offensiveness in order to achieve this end. That's what Nil By Mouth are doing with the word 'Tims'.

Everyone knows full well that 'Huns' just refers to Rangers and Neo-Gers; The People might not like the term, but there it is. In the same way, 'Tims' refers to Celtic and its supporters. When Nil By Mouth throw it into the mix, the hope is that somebody, somewhere, will claim to be offended by it. Everyone can then point the finger and shout, 'See! See! You don't like it. And if 'Tims' is sectarian, then so is 'Huns'!' So far this ploy seems not to have worked.

Nil By Mouth probably think they are on safer ground when they point out that calling Rangers/Neo-Gers supporters 'Orange bastards' is a sectarian slur against Protestants.[7] This claim itself, however, is a slur against the many Protestants that attend their respective churches and don't hate anyone because they go to a different place of worship. In fact, many Church of Scotland ministers often swap places with a local priest and they preside over each other's church service. Obviously the minister won't want to take part in any of ceremonial parts of the Mass, but they can lead the hymn singing and prayers and give a sermon. (And usually their sermons are a lot better than the ones the priests give. I suppose they're more practised at it!)

The simple fact is that The People sing Orange songs and align themselves, and their club, with the Orange Order. They can hardly complain, then, if, bastards or not, they get called 'Orange'!

The responsive insult to the Celtic support is 'Fenian bastards'. Fenians was the name given to Irish Republicans in the Nineteenth and early Twentieth Century. The Fenian Brotherhood was actually an American organisation, named after the legendary Fianna, a group of dedicated Irish warriors. It eventually came to denote all Irish Republicans. Since a lot of Celtic supporters sing about Ireland and Irish Republicanism then it seems quite apposite to use the term. It's not, however, as simple as that.

Throughout the Twentieth Century the word 'Fenian' has been used as a derogatory term for Irish Catholics. In Scotland it has long been employed to refer to anyone of the Roman Catholic faith, no matter where they might have originated. It is an insult and has always been intended as such. Centuries of propaganda in Scotland about Roman Catholicism being alien and insidious were behind this bigotry. All Catholics were viewed with suspicion in much the same way as Muslims are nowadays.

The song 'The Billy Boys' celebrates a gang of thugs, led by one Billy Fullerton, who came from Bridgeton in Glasgow. Apologists will claim that the line 'Up tae wur knees in Fenian blood' refers to Irish Republicans but this is disingenuous. An Italian ice-cream seller was just as likely to be set upon by Fullerton and his gang as an Irish labourer; the hatred was against Catholics, not just Irish Republicans. Unfortunately, that is still the case. Anyone in any doubt only needs to hear the renditions of 'No Pope of Rome' that accompany 'The Billy Boys' to realise that the hatred is directed against Catholics in general.

Of course, the particular hatred of the Irish is still given an airing, especially through the strains of a relatively new ditty, 'The Famine Song'. This unpleasant refrain is all about urging the descendants of Irish immigrants to 'go home'. Again, excuses are made, insisting that the song is meant to be a humorous piss-take on the celebration of Irish heritage by Celtic supporters. The fact that the song is also sung by Orange bands in Scotland and Northern Ireland tends to undermine this argument somewhat.

79

Nil By Mouth even tries to rewrite history in a desperate attempt at 'balance'. On its website, the charity outlines a brief history of sectarianism in Scotland, including the following observation:

Employment opportunities were denied to people of both denominations on the grounds of the religious group to which they belonged or were perceived and prejudged to belong. Discriminatory recruitment practices were conducted both officially and unofficially and a name considered traditionally Protestant or Catholic, or whether a candidate attended a Catholic or non-denominational school, was sufficient grounds for many businesses to exclude people from employment.[8]

This is utter crap. I contacted Nil By Mouth to ask where the evidence was to back up these statements. As I pointed out, it's easy to find old job advertisement announcing that 'RCs need not apply' but I, personally, have never seen any such proscription against Protestants. I was quite prepared to keep an open mind, as you are meant to as an historian, and accept that perhaps such evidenced did, in fact, exist. A spokesperson got back to me with the following reply:

Drawing on our experiences over the last 15 years we have seen and been told about numerous instances of sectarianism in the workplace - which have impacted on people from both religious traditions and none.
Probably the most relevant area of employment for you to look into for whatever piece of research you are doing is the area of education and the consistent practice of non-Catholics being overlooked and excluded from holding senior teaching and leadership posts at publicly funded schools.

This was nonsense and I told him so. In fact, I went further and accused him of using the same language of sectarian bigotry as the Orange Order. Again, I asked for historical evidence of Protestants being discriminated against in their search for employment. This time he had this to say:

Since 2003 there have been over 7,000 arrests for religiously aggravated offences in Scotland with thousands of individual

Catholics and Protestants being on the receiving end. Many of these incidents have occurred in workplaces. Nil by Mouth will continue to work with people of all faiths and none to tackle this blight.

He also provided me with a link to a story about some guy, a Protestant, having a couple of ribs broken when a spade was whacked across his shoulder blades. It was at this point that I gave up. It was
obvious that the issue I was highlighting was being avoided and the blatant lie about the history of sectarianism in Scotland is still there on
the website for all to see. It suggests to me that Nil By Mouth is part of the problem, not the solution.

The constant attempts to drag Celtic supporters into the debate and claim that both sets of fans are 'as bad as each other' in effect lends a certain legitimacy to The People's songs of sectarian bigotry and racism. Whether this is a conscious decision or not is irrelevant; it means that any opposition to these songs is shouted down and stifled. Worse; those complaining about the songs are often accused of being bigots themselves!

Such were the accusations levelled against Stan Collymore on Twitter, along with the usual death threats. BT Sports, meanwhile, was inundated with demands that Collymore be sacked.[9] Failure to comply was apparently going to result in thousands of subscriptions being cancelled. No doubt threats of violence were included as well, as they always are.

Just like the Sun did with the serialisation of Phil Mac Giolla Bhain's book, BT Sports gave in to the bullying threats. Neo-Gers played Raith Rovers at Starks Park on Friday 20th February and Collymore was dropped from the commentating team by BT Sports.[10] As The People celebrated their 'victory' on Twitter and other social media, Collymore and BT Sports parted company for good. According to BT Sports it was Collymore's decision not to work for them again.[11]

During the match at Starks Park Collymore's claims were pretty much vindicated as all the bigoted and racist bile came pouring out. Added to the mix was a bit of chanting about Collymore himself. It was claimed, especially by Collymore, that the chant was, 'Black Fenian bastard' but this was denied emphatically.

The evidence suggests that they were, in fact, singing, 'wife-beating bastard'; this in itself, though, was remarkably ironic, as Collymore pointed out. Paul Gascoigne was also a wife beater and yet he's idolised by The People.[12]

Newspaper journalists were quick to condemn the apparent censorship of Collymore and the unwillingness of our authorities to take proper action. As usual, however, they fell into the same, old trap of claiming that it was an 'Old Firm' problem. Daniel Taylor in the Guardian pointed out how the Ibrox hordes were polluted with a 'fog of bigotry' and that 'anyone who has a go will quickly find the hate mob unleashed on them.' He went on, however, 'maybe it would have been a more effective petition (the one Collymore asked everyone to sign) if it addressed both Old Firm clubs rather than just one.'[13]

Euan McLean in the Daily Record joined the ranks of The People in turning on Collymore. It was 'a case of right message, wrong guy,' he said. And, apparently, he found it hard to square all the hatred Collymore was exposing with the way Glasgow 'earned worldwide praise last summer for the friendliness of its people during its staging of the Commonwealth Games.'[14] Maybe he should have had a look at some of the Neo-Gers blogs, where they all roundly cursed the Games, or paid heed to the stories about the Commonwealth Games mascots being vandalised and stolen.[15]

McLean did admit that there was a problem with sectarian bigotry; but he made the mistake, as many do, of viewing this as purely a Glasgow problem. He also, as many do as well, dragged Celtic and its support into the debate. He spoke of folk 'who sing about fenian blood or those who glorify murders of innocent law abiding civilians in the name of a cause that has absolutely nothing to do with football?'[16] He doesn't mention Celtic specifically there but it's fairly obvious from the context that it's Celtic he's talking about.

Ironically, McLean mentions 'whataboutery' in his article; even though he is obviously indulging in it himself. The accusation he levels at Celtic supporters, moreover, is a rather insulting one; nobody glorifies 'murders of innocent law abiding civilians'. It's pretty clear, though, what he's referring to: the minority of folk among the Celtic support that sings and chants about the IRA.

It's an old saying, but no less true for it, that one man's terrorist is another man's freedom fighter. Nelson Mandela was considered a terrorist by the regime that imprisoned him and by Margaret Thatcher and her government, for that matter. Resistance groups in Nazi-occupied countries were no doubt viewed as terrorist organisations by the Germans and their allies in government. Whether or not somebody is a 'terrorist' all depends on your own, political point of view.

As for 'murders of innocent law abiding civilians', this accusation could easily be levelled at the British armed forces, and not just in the distant past. Recent operations in the Middle East have led to the deaths of many innocent civilians but, then, I suppose a few less 'darkies' in the world doesn't matter to some people.

It's like on the news when you get some overseas tragedy, such as a train crash in India. They'll always tell you first about the two British tourists that suffered a chipped incisor and a bruised big toe before they let you know about the two hundred Indian folk that died in the accident. In many ways we haven't moved all that far since the Nineteenth Century.

Also culpable in the killing of innocent civilians are the numerous Loyalist groups that abound in Northern Ireland. Again, how these groups are viewed depends on one's politics. A minority of the Ibrox support sing and chant about these organisations, just as a minority of Celtic supporters do with the IRA etc.

In this sense the argument that 'each side' is as bad as the other actually holds true. Both sets of fans contain a minority that sing and chant in support of proscribed organisations, whom the British Government views as terrorists. And it *is* a minority of both sets of supporters. You'd need to strain your ears to the limit to hear them if you're watching on television or listening to a radio broadcast. You only find out that they're there if somebody videos them on their phone and posts it on YouTube.

Evidence that it's a minority that indulges in this singing and chanting can be seen in the way folk try to claim that innocuous songs are, in fact, glorifying 'terrorism'. There have been accusations that 'The Bouncy', an Ibrox favourite, refers to a Catholic man being murdered by Loyalists, who jumped up and down on his head. A more ridiculous argument arose when Celtic supporters were singing,

'Having a party when Rangers die'. As well as jelly and ice-cream, this particular party was also going to have 'Pass the parcel when Rangers die'. Some demented souls tried to make out that this referred to parcel bombs! At any rate, it certainly shows up as false any claims that the majority of Celtic or Neo-Gers supporters indulge in such singing.

Remove these minorities from the equation and you are left with the fact that The People are on their own when it comes to sectarian and racist singing. And it's certainly not a minority when it comes to these songs; the noise is deafening as thousands join in with gusto. Unfortunately, as Stan Collymore discovered, even though The People are the only ones indulging in racist and sectarian bigotry, you are not allowed to mention this in Scotland. Celtic always has to be mentioned, even though their supporters are innocent of the charge levelled.

The excuse of the Scottish football authorities for doing nothing about this is that the club is doing all it can to stamp out bigotry among the support.[17] This was an integral part of the statement by the Rangers Supporters Trust against Stan Collymore. 'Rangers have done significantly more than most other clubs, including Mr Collymore's Celtic, to deal with issues around fans' behaviour over the years and we are sure that will continue.'[18] But is that really the case?

A common sight at every sports event in the world is someone making the sign of the cross as they get ready to take part. Whether it be tennis, athletics, swimming, basketball, or any other sport, many sportsmen and sportswomen do it as a matter of course, with nobody else having the least problem with it. Football is no different in this respect and you'll see players blessing themselves at every stadium on the planet. Well, that's not strictly true. There is one backward place where it is actively discouraged.

Ever since Rangers started its high-profile signing of Catholics in the late 1980s stories have emerged of players being told not to bless themselves. Marco Negri claimed in an Italian newspaper that this happened to him,[19] while others made the same kind of accusations and condemned the anti-Catholic culture at Ibrox.[20] Even Javier Hernandez was apparently advised not to go through his ritual prayer when Manchester United visited Ibrox.[21] In fact, he was put on the bench and didn't come onto the pitch until the seventy-sixth minute, just to make sure.

The new club continued this policy; at least according to Fran Sandaza it did. He told a Spanish newspaper that 'on my first day I was advised not to cross myself before matches.'[22] Neo-Gers, of course, denied the accusation emphatically. But, surely, all those players down through the years weren't lying?

The People, however, aren't just renowned for being anti-Catholic; there are the anti-Irish sentiments that they constantly express as well. What have Rangers and Neo-Gers done to stamp out this particular bigotry? Sadly, the answer is not a lot. In fact, every time a match takes place at Ibrox a little piece of anti-Irish bigotry is blasted out over the PA system.

Every team's supporters avow that they would follow their heroes to the ends of the earth; to Hell and back, if need be. Rangers, and Neo-Gers, fans feel the same and one of the official club songs reflects that fact. There's a line in the song 'Follow, Follow' that expresses just how far they would go to support their team: 'If we go to Dublin, we will follow on.' Why Dublin? The answer's obvious; it's the last place on earth that any one of them would ever want to go. And why's that? Because they hate Ireland so much, that's why! And this is a song that the club itself condones and plays on match days.

This song might seem pretty harmless *per se*, but taken in the context of the sectarian and racist bigotry endemic among the Ibrox support, it appears much more suspicious. Rather than try to stamp out the anti-Irish racism of The People, the club is actually encouraging it.

One of the arguments against The People being racist is the notion that being anti-Irish is not racist at all. Bill McMurdo, in discussing the prison sentence meted out to David Limond, brother of the television comedian, for his abuse of Angela Haggerty, summed up the idea succinctly.

> Limond was told that his attacks on Miss Haggerty were racist because he made anti-Irish remarks in relation to her. Now, I don't know Limond's ethnic background but, like most Scots, I am sure he could find some Irish ancestry in his make-up. Since you cannot be racist against your own race, this charge looks pretty invalid.[23]

This argument is pretty ridiculous when you think about it. Historically, the Irish were looked down on as a lesser people, not as advanced or civilised as the folk of Scotland and England. They were something *other*, not fit for anything but manual labour, so long as it was not too taxing mentally. The very idea that anyone from the civilised part of the British Isles might be related to these semi-humans would fill most Englishmen and Scotsmen with abject terror. It was the gentlefolk of mainland Britain that portrayed the Irish as a lower race, not the Irish themselves. Many of The People still cling to these beliefs while the rest of the world has moved on.

As well as just about everybody in Scotland being able to find an Irishman or two among their ancestors, they would also find other interesting folk in their family trees if they went back far enough. *Homo Sapiens* originally came from Africa, according to experts, so, ultimately, it must be impossible to be racist at all since the whole world is interrelated. Go back even further and we should all be inviting our simian cousins round for a cup of PG Tips!

And we wouldn't just find the odd Irishman among our antecedents, most, if not all, Scots would also find a few English folk swinging from the branches of our family trees. With that in mind, it must be impossible for anyone that is Scottish to be racist against the English. Not according to McMurdo. During the Scottish independence referendum, he spoke of 'racist Nats' as he lambasted the SNP for supposedly being anti-English.[24]

Speaking of the SNP brings us neatly to an example of how two-faced our media can be. During the Scottish independence referendum arguments got quite heated and quite a few bams on both sides dished out abuse online. Nicola Sturgeon and Alex Salmond received death threats but our media didn't want to know about it. Instead, they invented a mythical, organised rabble they called 'Cybernats'. Abuse suffered by 'YES' campaigners, both online and on the streets, was by-and-large ignored as our media rushed headlong to condemn the 'Cybernats'. Of course, their agenda was obvious; they didn't agree with those campaigning for independence so went all-out to vilify them.

It's a different story when it comes to the issue of sectarianism, though. Everyone knows who is to blame but nobody in our media will come out and say it. Is this because they actually support the sectarian bigotry of The People? In some cases, yes, but mostly it's fear that drives the necessity of having to drag Celtic and its supporters into things. There's certainly the fear of losing what they perceive to be the majority of their audience, even though the majority in Scotland are completely against the bigotry of The People. There's also the fear of the violent backlash that would be unleashed if our media was actually to tell the truth.

Ironically, the SNP are caught in the same trap, afraid of alienating voters and riling up The People into violent acts. That's why the Offensive Behaviour at Football and Threatening Communications (Scotland) Act is aimed at Celtic supporters as well as The People.

Still, all this argument is, ultimately, futile, since nobody wants to discuss it. The Scottish media just goes into the default position, fingers in ears and repeating the mantra, 'Both as bad as each other. Both as bad as each other…' Anyone that tries to tackle the real issue of anti-Catholic and anti-Irish bigotry soon finds himself under attack, as Stan Collymore did. Soon, the whole thing is swept under the carpet again and everyone pretends that it doesn't exist.

The endemic opinion among many in our country, including those in the media, is possibly summed up by our old friend Jabba. In 2008, while writing about 'The Famine Song,' Traynor had this to say:

> So, to all those, of any religion or race, who think Scotland is such a bad, twisted place full of bigots and racists there is only one thing to say. Go. Go on, just gather up your prejudices, take your suspicions and pack your loathing of Scotland. Go find a better place to live and leave us to get on with the job of making something good of this country.[25]

11
You Need Hands

On the night of 13th February, while Neo-Gers were being beaten 2-0 by Hibs and Bomber Brown was out in the street shouting about rats, the Daily Record's Gary Ralston thought it would be a wizard wheeze to watch the match from the dear seats. He dressed up as a caricature of a gangster, complete with Charlie Endell-style camel coat. It was obvious to everyone who this particular little charade was aimed at. This was confirmed the next day when his giggly article appeared in the Record, in which he claimed that Sandy Easdale was giving him the evil eye. The photographs accompanying the piece, however, showed that Sandy couldn't have cared less.[1]

The reason for this jolly jape was that the Daily Record had been banned from Ibrox. As he desperately tried to stifle the titters, Ralston claimed that it was 'game, set and match to Record Sport'. As usual, though, the Daily Record was congratulating itself for doing nothing much. Ralston had been invited to Ibrox by some of the more well-heeled among The People; it's unclear, however, who paid for the ticket. Did Ralston really imagine that the skint Neo-Gers board would throw out a paying customer? Rather than getting one up on the Neo-Gers board, Ralston was actually helping to keep the lights on for a short while.

The ban itself was hardly a surprise; except, of course, to the Daily Record. No specific reason was given for the ban. All that was said was that it was due to 'recent reporting by your journalists in the Daily Record'.[2] Rather ridiculously, the Record claimed that they had been banned 'because we told the truth.'[3] More likely it was because the Record had spent months vilifying the Neo-Gers board, while beating the drum for a criminal from South Africa.

In the run-up to the EGM the bile thrown at Ashley and the Neo-Gers board by our media grew in volume and intensity. They were all desperate to get the Real Rangers Men onboard and it looked like they were finally going to get their wish. The rest of us waited for Mike Ashley to rouse himself from his slumber and swat the lot of them, like so many irritating bluebottles. It was going to be a bloodbath!

As the 6th of March drew nearer, the more excited Keith Jackson and his colleagues got. The resignation of James Easdale on the 25th of February got them frothing at the mouth,[4] while Chairman David Somers doing walking away on 2nd March made them positively orgasmic.[5] It looked as if 'The Real Rangers Men' were 'coming down the road'.

Even God was on the side of Dave King and his cronies. Reverend Stuart MacQuarrie, who seems to be some kind of unofficial chaplain at Ibrox, came out to blast the Neo-Gers board with hellfire and brimstone. He said:

> It is unusual for someone who is a Church of Scotland minister to enter publicly into the rights and wrongs of a boardroom battle such as that at Rangers. However, I cannot stand idly by as people's lives and livelihoods are considered mere pawns in a corporate power struggle, discarded as being of no further use.[6]

Strangely, this man of God's sympathy didn't extend to all those that were swindled when Rangers was liquidated and the Big Lie was introduced to pretend that Rangers still existed. It seems that only The People are deserving of such sympathy! And the good Reverend made sure he kept up the pretence by saying:

> When Rangers went into administration, it was the ordinary fan who scrimped, saved and donated money to the Rangers Fighting Fund. It was the ordinary fan who invested their hard-earned cash in shares when the club was re-floated.[7]

No mention, of course, of liquidation. He went on:

> The trust which has been abused will only be restored with the election as directors of people who know, understand and love Rangers – such as Dave King, John Gilligan, Paul Murray and the Three Bears. They have character, part of the DNA of being a Ranger.[8]

89

Dave King? A convicted criminal? This deluded minister seems to think that this is a worthy person; a person with 'character'. Then again, since he sees nothing wrong with all those creditors being robbed then it stands to reason that he's going to endorse a crook to be in charge of the new club.

And so it came to pass that God took His place among the shareholders on 6th March, with Bomber Brown, King, the Three Bears and even Sooperally. He looked upon the five empty seats on the podium and saw that it was good.

In fact, the five empty seats were soon reduced to two, as somebody came out and removed three of them, to the cheers and catcalls of the crowd. There were only two board members left, Llambias and Leach, so why they put five chairs out in the first place was a mystery. Perhaps it was to provide a bit of theatre for the papers, who obligingly reported it.[9]

Llambias and Leach never turned up and the two seats were taken by Football admin boss Andrew Dickson and company secretary Matthew Wood, with Dickson chairing the meeting. There were about five hundred shareholders at the meeting, all rooting for King and the Three Bears. When the vote came, Llambias and Leach were ousted from the board and Dave King, Paul Murray and John Gilligan were elected onto it. The whole thing was an anti-climax with not a voice raised against King & Co. Even Sandy Easdale didn't turn up, all the shareholders he held proxies for abstaining from the vote. The first act of the new board was to appoint Douglas Park, a man who always looks as if he's sucking a pickled onion, as a director.[10] The Real Rangers Men were where they'd wanted to be since 2012; in charge of Neo-Gers.

Of course, the mood was triumphant, with King standing on the steps afterwards, talking about new starts and glorious futures. The real triumphant rejoicing, however, came on the 10th of March, the first match at Ibrox since that beating by Hibs on the 13th of February. It was the first home game with the new board in charge and everyone was expecting great things, even though the previous Saturday had seen a dull, goalless draw against Cowdenbeath at Central Park.

The Directors' Box was filled to overflowing with all those that had been championing the Real Rangers Men over the last three years. Chris 'Ze List' Graham was there, as was Halloweeen

Houston, Bomber Brown and even a big, scary-looking creature that turned out to be Mark Dingwall, who runs the Follow Follow website. John Greig decided that it was time to return to Ibrox and took his place right at the very back, apparently not keen on getting involved in all the celebration and back-slapping.[11]

Seated at the front was a surprise: David Leggat, who many of us thought had shuffled off this mortal coil or, at least, shuffled off to some anonymous pub in Lanarkshire. Malcolm Murray sat not too far from Leggat, keeping a sharp lookout for video cameras and swearing to anyone that would listen that the smell of booze was coming from Leggat and not him.[12]

Walter Smith appeared in order to lend a little dignity to the proceedings but his protégé was notable by his absence. Nobody had done more to help the Real Rangers Men than Fifth Columnist Sooperally and yet, it seemed, he hadn't been invited. Then again, maybe he was but was too busy seeing to his tatties; an overnight frost had been forecast. It looked as if Keith Jackson's invitation had got lost in the post, while Big Jabba was left out as well.

The occupants of the Directors' Box took the cheers of the crowd and then sat, straight-backed, surveying the stadium and team that they now purported to own. They were like the Politburo of the old Soviet Union, looking over the annual May Day parade. And the similarities didn't end there. Most of the tanks and missiles that used to trundle along Red Square were empty hulks; an illusion of might. In the same way, the stadium surrounding the Directors' Box was falling to pieces while the team was a poor imitation of the old Rangers.

'The resilience of Queen of the South was enough to earn them a point at Ibrox,' said the BBC report,[13] but that was being far too generous to Neo-Gers. If anything Queens would have considered it two points lost rather than a point gained. Neo-Gers were abysmal and left the field to a now-familiar sound: the booing of the crowd.

Again, the only positive aspect of the Neo-Gers team was Haris Vuckic, who was proving to be a class act. Unfortunately, this emphasised the fact that the other four loan players from Newcastle were about as useful as a holy-water font in the Ibrox tunnel. Vuckic was the only one that was actually fit enough to play.

Remie Streete, who sounds like a TV detective, limped off injured in the first half of that Scottish Cup game against Raith Rovers, you'll remember. On top of his thigh injury, Streete had been plagued with an ear infection and hadn't appeared since that one game.[14] Shane Ferguson also suffered from a long-term condition, having been out with a knee injury for months.[15] Kevin Mbabu, meanwhile, had been hit with a groin injury and had already been out for a couple of months he was signed up for Neo-Gers. He said in February that he hoped to be fit soon and make it into the Neo-Gers first team.[16] He didn't.

The fifth member of the group, Gael Bigirimana, had no injury to speak of but was unfit for duty nonetheless. He was suffering from some mystery illness that was baffling medical science. Experts were sent in from the World Health Organisation but nobody seemed to be able to determine what was wrong with him. All we learned was that he definitely didn't have Hepatitis C. The Daily Record, being what it is, decided that the SFA was to blame.[17]

A thousand quid a week each this shower was costing Neo-Gers. It was one more thing to hold against Ashley. Then again, Vuckic was probably the best player in the team and £5k a week was a lot less than some of the duds in the Neo-Gers line-up were pocketing. Little wonder, then, that not too much fuss was made about the sickbed quartet; Vuckic alone was worth all that money.

In the meantime, the new Neo-Gers board appointed Stuart McCall, who had left Motherwell in November, as caretaker manager until the end of the season.[18] Kenny McDowall left his post with immediate effect, going to join his boss in that garden where the paths are paved with gold.

McCall's resignation from Mothewell had come as

something of a surprise. Yes, things had been going badly and the supporters had begun to turn on McCall but, in the main, he was expected to turn things around.[19] Shouting for the manager to go is always the knee-jerk reaction of supporters and, quite often, they simply mean it as a metaphorical kick up the arse for him to make some changes. Nobody really expected him to walk away.

Of course, this sudden resignation prompted speculation that McCall was being lined up to replace the man with the green fingers at Ibrox. Such speculation seemed more credible when Sooperally handed in his own resignation in December; McCall, however, refused to comment on the subject.[20] And now here he was in charge at Ibrox, thanks to the Real Rangers Men. It made you wonder if he was a part of their plans all along. There were rumours that he had knocked back the chance to manage St Mirren[21], which, if true, would show that he was waiting for something.

It was a bit of a kick in the teeth for Sooperally, who had practically given up his managerial career in the cause of the Real Rangers Men. But, then, he didn't appear to be too bothered so maybe he'd been in on things; he was certainly being rewarded financially. And, of course, he could always go back on the TV; all he needed was a shave.

The People were excited at the prospect of having a new manager and over 35,000 of them turned up to see Neo-Gers take on Livingston. That might not seem like a lot but it was one of the biggest crowds seen at Ibrox for a long time. Unfortunately, the match ended in a miserable 1-1 draw so 7,000 fewer attended three days later against Alloa. That game finished up a draw as well; 2-2 was the final score. It looked as if, despite the new board and new manager, nothing much had changed with the Neo-Gers team.

That would explain why it was hardly a capacity crowd at Easter Road on 22nd March; that and the fact that Hibs

had won the last three encounters comfortably. McCall decided to make some tactical changes; something that Sooperally had always steadfastly refused to do. He packed the midfield to disrupt Hibs' game. It wasn't pretty but it certainly did the trick. Neo-Gers won 2-0.[22]

The first goal was a lucky deflection, while the second one was a Kenny Miller special: one of his team-mates fouls an opposition player and Miller nips in and scores

while everyone's preoccupied with the referee, who refuses to give a free kick. But when did that ever stop The People from claiming that it was a magnificent victory? They were coming down the road – again!

The Daily Record, of course, joined in the jubilation, stating, rather ridiculously, that Neo-Gers had 'humbled Hibs at Easter Road'.[23] From the triumphalist tone of the Record's article you'd have thought that Neo-Gers were now on course to challenge Hearts for the Championship title. The truth was, however, that Hibs losing to Neo-Gers meant that Hearts could now no longer be caught. They had secured the only automatic promotion available and the best that Neo-Gers could hope for now was to come second and reach the Premiership via the play-offs.

The euphoria continued to the end of March with a 4-1 drubbing of Cowdenbeath at Ibrox. Once again, Haris Vuckic was the star of the show, proving that he was worth the money being spent on him and his comrades. He was not praised too much by the Neo-Gers website, though; nobody wanted to admit that their best player had arrived courtesy of Mike Ashley![24]

The new board at Ibrox, meanwhile, had settled in, with Paul Murray acting as interim chairman. Dave King had disappeared back to South Africa to await a decision on whether or not he was a 'fit and proper person'. This was hardly a formality, no matter how good a spin King tried to put on it. The SFA was one thing, but the London Stock Exchange had its own stringent rules, which it would enforce without fear or favour.

Llambias and Leach were suspended, pending an investigation to see if they could be removed permanently. With James Easdale already gone, the Real Rangers Men were free to fill the boardroom with their own appointees. Paul Murray, Douglas Park and John Gilligan were elected onto the board at the EGM. Andrew Dickson was kept on as football administrator, while James Blair, a solicitor of long standing was made Company Secretary. Also joining the board was John Bennett, a fund manager and one of the original Blue Knights.[25] The boardroom hadn't been that full in ages.

James Blair was a member of Rangers First and had been acting as their legal advisor and representative,[26] prompting suspicions that directorships were being handed out as rewards. It certainly appeared that way when Chris Graham, of all people, was appointed to the board.[27] When asked for a statement, Graham said, 'Und now, ve shall examine Ze List!'

While we all waited to see if Bomber Brown, Halloween Houston and Auld Leggat were offered similar sinecures, a question should have been asked that wasn't; where was the money coming from to pay for this shower? Presumably, none of these directors was working for nothing and it was ironic that they all had their snouts in the trough after accusing the previous board of being 'rats' and 'parasites'. The irony was compounded by the fact that the Easdales had actually taken nothing out of

94

Neo-Gers.

As soon as he was appointed, Chris 'Ze List' Graham went through his online accounts, deleting practically everything he had ever written. Unfortunately for him, he seemed not to have realised that people could, and did, take screenshots of his posts. They now came back to haunt him.

One of the worst of his posts on Twitter was made on the day of the murder of the Charlie Hebdo cartoonists. While everyone condemned the murders, some people also condemned the implicit racism displayed in the magazine. If you try to stir up hatred, it's hardly surprising if it ends in violence. When a Muslim preacher expressed his concerns about Charlie Hebdo, Listy Graham responded with a cartoon of his own. Whether the rough drawing was his own work or somebody else's, it couldn't be denied that it was Graham that posted it. The drawing depicted what was meant to be the Prophet Mohammed, on his knees, giving a handjob to Jar Jar Binks from the Star Wars films. Of course, there were immediate calls for Neo-Gers to sack him.[28]

And so, just three days after he was appointed, Graham had to resign from the Neo-Gers board.[29] The next day Graham made a statement apologising for the Tweet. He told the Daily Record:

> Freedom of speech is one of the foundations that our country is built upon. However, with that freedom comes a responsibility to be sensitive to the views of all our nation's communities. This tweet did not do that. For that I apologise unreservedly.[30]

There are accusations that Graham has a long history of sectarian and racist abuse; 'Ze List' itself is proof of that. The mass deletion of his online posts means that there's not much more in the way of evidence; unless, of course there are other screenshots lurking out there. It also means that there's nothing to back up this part of his statement to the Record: 'I also tweeted my support for the Muslim community during exchanges that day'.[31] Somehow I doubt that.

And so the Real Rangers Men were dragged into a scandal almost before they'd got a chance to get their coats off. It hardly augured well that they had appointed a proven sectarian bigot onto the board; perhaps it was their way of saying that it was 'still Rangers'! Graham rounded off his statement by saying, 'I am extremely proud to have played a part in helping Rangers to secure regime change'.[32]

Jar Jar Binks, meanwhile, was unavailable for comment.

12
<u>Something Else</u>

As they had threatened to do, WH Ireland resigned as the Nominated Adviser (NOMAD) on the 4th March, as soon as it looked as if the Real Rangers Men were going to triumph at the EGM. This meant that Neo-Gers was immediately suspended from the AIM Stock Exchange. Not that King seemed to be too bothered; he had already made it plain that he'd intended to get rid of WH Ireland as soon as possible anyway.[1]

Stock Exchange rules say that a company can't trade on its market if it doesn't have a NOMAD. Neo-Gers had a month to get one, otherwise it would be kicked off the AIM Exchange permanently. Honest Dave assured everyone that there was nothing to worry about; he already had a NOMAD lined up.[2] The People and the institutional investors could vote for his coup with complete confidence.

As we know, they did vote for King and his merry band, believing that having Real Rangers Men at the top of the marble staircase would solve all the problems at the club. Ever since the new club started many of The People had been desperate to see such a scenario. The trouble was that nobody thought beyond that. Getting Real Rangers Men into the Blue Room had become an end in itself and, now that it had been achieved, nobody was quite sure what was going to happen next.

The supporters of Mike Ashley were disappointed at how easily he seemed to have rolled over. The fact was, though, that Ashley still had Neo-Gers tightly by the bollocks; the board owed Sports Direct five million quid and he'd be going nowhere until he got it back. Indeed, Neo-Gers might have to go crawling to Ashley before the month was out; there was a hefty wage bill to settle, including the salary of the club's gardener. Ashley could still win out after all. Despite hopes that he might call in his loan after Llambias and Leach were sacked, in breach of the loan agreement,[3] Ashley still did nothing.

It was beginning to look as if Phil Mac Giolla Bhain's theory about Ashley was correct. On more than one occasion Mac Giolla Bhain had put forward the idea that Ashley wasn't in the least bit interested in running a football club; his efforts to get rid of Newcastle United seemed to confirm this. He had what he wanted from Neo-Gers, the advertising and the retail business; somebody else could have the hassle of being in charge of the club and its crumbling stadium.[4]

Mac Giolla Bhain was making an excellent point and even the most fervent supporter of Ashley couldn't deny that he'd actually put no money into the club; apart, of course, from loans. If things weren't going to get better overnight with the Real Rangers Men in charge, they certainly couldn't get any worse! Or could they?

Keith Jackson, of the Daily Record, appeared to think that things were going to improve. In the middle of March, Jackson attended a conference in Melbourne, Australia, which went by the grand name of the '2015 Money in Sport Conference'. Jackson was there to tell the good folks at the conference about all the troubles at Ibrox. Helpfully, the Daily Record provided a video of Jackson's performance.[5]

He recounted all the woes that The People had gone through since 2011, when Craig Whyte appeared on the scene. He omitted, of course, the part he himself had played in cheerleading for the billionaire with 'wealth off the radar'. (He also omitted to tell the audience that his 'expert' status depended on nicking his 'exclusives' from bloggers, especially Phil Mac Giolla Bhain!) He brought his narrative up to date with the observation that Neo-Gers was 'finally in the hands of people who care for it'. His analysis seemed to suggest that everything was going to be alright now; as long as they managed to get rid of Mike Ashley.

There is a point in the video where Jackson visibly squirms. His narrative reaches the point when Charlie Green bought the assets and started up Neo-Gers. Despite Jackson's assertion that Green 'bought the club', the Australian host is clear that the old club had died and that Green's club was a new one. 'That's a prickly subject,' says Jackson, but it's not such for the host and his audience. It's clear that 'legally', as the host says, liquidation means death and the current entity can only be a new club.

Jackson effectively ignores this and moves on, albeit in a clear state of discomfort.

The People were angered by this performance, feeling that Jackson didn't stand up robustly enough to this challenge to the Big Lie. Remarkably, one phrase that was used was, 'If you tell a lie often enough ...'[6] And there wasn't a shred of irony in this declaration! Did they really expect the whole world's press to fall into line as easily as the media in Scotland?

And that wasn't all. Jackson had the gall to say that it probably was in the spirit of sporting integrity that Neo-Gers was placed in the bottom tier. Even though he regurgitated the old myths of Armageddon and financial suicide, The People were blazing;[7] with them it is all or nothing. Keith really should have stayed at home. All he had achieved was making the Scottish media look ridiculous by trying to perpetuate the Big Lie and angering The People by not punching the Australian host for saying that the new club *was* a new club!

While Keith Jackson was making an arse of himself in Australia, the new board at Neo-Gers was searching for a new NOMAD. Well, ostensibly they were looking but nobody could be entirely sure. Honest Dave was actually on record as stating, 'In a perfect world, my personal preference for the rebuilding of Rangers my choice would be not listed. But it is listed. And I'm going to say that *unfortunately* it's listed.'[8] (My italics.) From that quote it's quite reasonable to infer that perhaps the search for a new NOMAD was not being executed altogether as rigorously as was being made out.

King also hinted at the possibility of de-listing, both immediately before and immediately after the EGM. On the 6th March he had this to say:

> I don't think we will be going to the City at this point. It would be very difficult given the history of Rangers' performance in the stock market to go to the City and ask people to produce funds from other people's money.
>
> Charles Green did a marvelous job of selling it to the City but I don't believe a football club should be bringing other people's money into it.
>
> It should be people like myself, who are willing to invest

while understanding the risk.[9]

Then, on the 9th of March, he stated:

> The advantage of not being listed is you don't spend all the money involved in being listed, but also you can do what you want with people you want to. If I want Douglas Park to join the board, he joins the board and I don't have to go to some chap in London who has to do an investigation and goes into something that happened 15 years ago.[10]

Could he have been any clearer about what his intentions were? King's preference wasn't all that might be holding things back. There were rumours that the folk that ran the AIM market weren't too keen on having Neo-Gers back trading. Keith Jackson, back from his jaunt down-under, pointed out that

> ...over this last year Rangers have the dubious honour of being tagged officially as the single most complained about company on AIM's books. There is a strong suspicion the top brass in the City are sick to the back teeth of this Ibrox odditorium.[11]

So, really, what was the point of looking for a NOMAD at all? King didn't want Neo-Gers trading on the Stock Exchange and the Stock Exchange didn't want Neo-Gers stinking up the place; why not just de-list straight away? The truth was that King had to be seen to be seeking a NOMAD and maintaining the place of Neo-Gers on the AIM, otherwise he would fail at the well-worn strategy used by everyone ever connected with Ibrox: blame somebody else. Those three words are probably engraved on the wall in the Blue Room and both King and Murray had been denizens of that hallowed chamber before.

King had already said, speaking of WH Ireland, that 'there was a complete lack of governance and transparency under its watch'.[12] Keith Jackson also pointed the finger at WH Ireland for resigning immediately instead of ensuring an orderly handover, effectively causing all the problems for the new board.[13] The implication was clear; the previous board had been a bunch of crooks, which might deter any NOMAD wanting to work for Neo-Gers. Any counter-argument stating that the previous board had no problem securing a NOMAD had already been answered; WH Ireland were crooks as well!

And so, when the deadline finally arrived on the 2nd April, the Real Rangers Men had their excuses all lined up. A statement was released, saying the following:

> The prospective Nomad completed its checks on the "fit and proper" status of the existing and the proposed additional director of the company and confirmed to the company that it was satisfied on both fronts.

It then carried out its own assessment of the company's profile over the last several years and the issues which had been encountered. We understand this process involved discussions with the exchange. We were advised that, following this process, the prospective Nomad was unable to take up appointment.

> We also understand that any alternative Nomad is liable to encounter similar difficulties and therefore the company requires to terminate its listing on AIM.[14]

Effectively, King had got what he wanted, de-listing from the AIM, while being able to blame the previous board. The plan now, apparently, was to trade on the ISDX market.[15] As everyone in our media was quick to point out, the ISDX was where Arsenal traded its shares. This was rather a ridiculous comparison; Neo-Gers was certainly no Arsenal! The plan was also disingenuous since they all must have known that a NOMAD was required to trade on the ISDX as well.[16]

This obvious deception must have had a reason and it did; in fact, more than one. Firstly, there was the business of King becoming a director. Nobody expected the SFA to put any obstacles in his way; the Stock Exchange, however, would be another matter entirely. The powers-that-be at the AIM couldn't care less about what was best for Neo-Gers, or, for that matter, Scottish football, which, to the SFA and our media was the same thing. All they'd be concerned about would be that a convicted crook shouldn't be running a PLC. With Neo-Gers no longer trading on the AIM, the Stock Exchange had no say in what went on at Ibrox. With no market to trade in, there was no need for anyone to be poking their nose in. All King needed to worry about now was Mr. Campbell Ogilvie EBT asking where he should sign.

The other, rather obvious, advantage to not being listed on a stock market was to do with that 'no need for anyone to poke their nose in' bit. With no rules and regulations to follow, there was no reason for anybody to know what was going on inside the Blue Room. There would also be no need for inconvenient matters, like AGMs, to get in the way of the board doing whatever it liked.[17]

Of course, the Real Rangers Men had always been in favour of transparency and accountability; but it wasn't their fault that things had changed. It was all down to the previous boards and their crooked NOMADS that Neo-Gers was now, effectively, a private company. This situation would come in handy for the new board; just so long as everyone was clear that it was all somebody else's fault.

The way things were had already proven useful when it came time to pay the wages at the end of March. Rather than go anywhere near the second tranche of Ashley's loan, the Three Bears stumped up the cash. This was an unsecured loan, to be repaid at the end of the year, 'which will provide the Company with time to deliver a longer term funding solution,' said a statement from the club.[18]

The long-term solution was obviously that much-promised investment that King had been going on about for three years. He still hadn't come up with it, even though he had promised that he would plough money in no matter what the outcome of his 'fit and proper' tests. He said that, 'if I am not passed as a fit and proper person then I will not sit on the board. I will still invest and be a supporter.'[19] So where was the money? Paul Murray told us at the end of March.

'To respect the processes, Dave will not be investing until we have him cleared by the SFA,' Murray announced. He explained why: 'One of the problems Sports Direct and Mike Ashley had was they actually went ahead and made an investment when they didn't have pre-clearance from the SFA and we don't want to get into that position again.'[20]

That, however, was utter pish. Nobody was interested in Ashley's investments at Ibrox; mainly because he didn't make any! He had tied the whole club up in knots with loans and controlled the boardroom through them; that was what had drawn the attention of the SFA.

King, or anybody else for that matter, was free to invest as much as they liked. Murray was, to put it bluntly, lying.

Really, what King was doing was blackmailing the SFA. Since 2012 our football authorities and our media have never tired of telling us that Scottish football is doomed unless Neo-Gers is in the top tier. Honest Dave was calling their bluff. If they didn't rubber-stamp him as being 'fit and proper' then it looked like he wouldn't be putting any money in. Was the SFA willing to risk the death of what they'd been telling us for nearly three years was Rangers?

Whatever the outcome with King, it seemed to be clear that all that had happened at Neo-Gers so far was swapping one lender for another; what wasn't clear were the amounts involved in this lending. Was the one-and-a-half-million quid made available by the Three Bears the full extent of the loan? Had facilities been made available for Neo-Gers to draw down more funds if required? After all, there was going to be another payday due in April. The truth was that nobody knew.

Business was being conducted behind closed doors and the boardroom could tell the media and the public any story they liked. De-listing meant that no outside agency had to be kept up to date with developments and it was striking that no other fans' representative had been appointed to replace that purveyor of pornography, Chris 'Ze List' Graham. Transparency and accountability were now even less in evidence than they had been previously; but, of course, it wasn't the fault of the Real Rangers Men.

It was an enviable position to be in. Neo-Gers could still be dependent upon loans with nobody any the wiser. We could all be told that King was pouring money in when the truth was completely different. The People were being kept even more in the dark than ever before. What was their reaction? Were they going to get the pishy bedsheets and rat traps out again?

A couple of comments on a Neo-Gers website probably summed up how most of The People felt:

> We have Gers men directing the club with more wisdom than I. Quite happy to let the suits take that lead and let punters like me concentrate on matters fitba.[21]
> Well said…as you said lets trust the lads that have taken control after all we put them their. Its Fitba we should be

talking about lets get behind the team onwards and upwards. I am sick of reading about politics on ifs and but's about the Rangers.[22]

The old 'onwards and upwards' mentality was certainly to the fore when Hearts came visiting on the 5th April. The Neo-Gers players lined up to applaud the champions onto the pitch; though, it has to be said, none of them looked particularly happy about it![23]

The match itself ended in a 2-1 victory for Neo-Gers, letting them leapfrog Hibs back into second place. It was hardly a great display, however, since Hearts' players probably already had half an eye on their summer holidays. Even then, the referee had to play his usual part in ensuring a Neo-Gers win.[24]

It was only a few days later that The People were brought back down to earth with a bump. Neo-Gers were trounced 3-0 by Queen of the South at Palmerston, sending them back into third place.[25] They still had a game in hand, though, so it wasn't all doom and gloom. In fact, The People, on reflection, were still optimistic.

A bad day at the office. QoS got the breaks and we didnt. Get over it. When we beat Raith on sunday and Hibs fail to beat Hearts everything will be fine again.[26]

13
Watcha Gonna Do About It?

At the end of March, the Neo-Gers interim financial results showed that the club was still leaking money, with losses of £2.6 million between June and December 2014. The Real Rangers Men were happy to let everyone see all this, since it reflected badly on the previous board. There was also a big surprise in the accounts. It turned out that Newcastle United was due a bonus of £500,000 if Neo-Gers were to win promotion to the Premiership.[1] That was a lot of cash for a bunch of invalids. It was probably time for ATOS to get involved! But there was even worse news waiting in the wings.

'Intellectual' is not a word one normally associates with Ibrox but, like most other companies, Neo-Gers has what is called 'intellectual property'. This includes things like the brand name, crests, mottos and the like. In the case of Neo-Gers, these included the RFC crest, the badges and the 'Ready' motto. In reality, this 'intellectual property' belonged to the old club but it was all part-and-parcel of the 'Big Lie' that Rangers hadn't died so Green's new club were assumed to own them now. Only, it didn't; not anymore.

The shocking news emerged in the second week of April: Mike Ashley was holding all the intellectual property as part of the security for his loan. As the Daily Record put it, he now had control of the 'club's crown jewels'.[2] Well, he certainly had the Real Rangers Men by the crown jewels. It was looking more and more as if King and his cronies weren't really in charge of much at all. Ashley even owned Broxi Bear!

The terms and conditions of the loan agreement, however, made it plain that all the IP rights would be returned as soon as the £5 million was repaid. Furthermore, Sports Direct had no right to sell goods with the 'Rangers' logos or trademarks, except through Rangers Retail, from which Neo-Gers would receive a quarter of the profits. Neither had Sports Direct any right to license the IP rights to any third party.[3] So there wasn't that much to worry about. All that needed to happen was for Ashley to get his money back; £5 million quid would be small change to the 'off-the-radar' wealth of Honest Dave and the Real Rangers Men.

Unfortunately, as we have already seen, King had no intention of putting any money into the club until he was passed as 'fit and proper'. The 'Three Bears', meanwhile, didn't seem to have the wherewithal to stump up enough cash to pay off Ashley. All any of them had managed to do so far was lend Neo-Gers enough to pay March's bills; no more than Sandy Easdale had done on more than one occasion. It looked like they were stuck with Ashley and Sports Direct.

On the pitch, things seemed to have improved for Neo-Gers and they came off the back of that defeat to Queen of the South to thump Raith Rovers 4-0 on the 12th April at Ibrox. This put them on equal points with Hibs but behind them on goal difference.[4] They still had that game in hand, though, and that would be against Livingston on Wednesday 15th. Livingston was struggling to avoid relegation so The People had every right to be confident as the end of the season drew nearer.

As it was, Neo-Gers struggled to get a 1-1 draw, with some good, old-fashioned 'honest mistakes' helping them out. Myles Hippolyte, the Livingston striker, scored in the seventh minute but the goal was chalked off for a foul that nobody else saw. Meanwhile, Vuckic elbowed an opposition player without receiving as much as a talking-to.[5] It was just like old times for The People.

As well as the SFA match officials doing their best for the Neo-Gers cause, the high-heid-yins in the SPFL decided to show a touch of bias as well. There were only three games left to play in the Championship and it looked as if things might go down to the wire. Neo-Gers were only one point ahead of Hibs and Falkirk were still challenging QOS for fourth place; the final day on the 2nd May was going to be an exciting one. And then the SPFL dropped its bombshell: Neo-Gers' last match against Hearts was going to take place on the Sunday, the 3rd.

Ostensibly, this move was all about the game being televised; Leeann Dempster, the Hibs Chief Executive, however, was outraged. Why should one team have the advantage of already knowing how their rivals for second place had done in their final game? Ann Budge at Hearts supported the complaint by Hibs and even decided to submit a formal complaint herself. Amazingly, the SPFL's answer was for the other teams to apply to move their matches to the Sunday![6]

The very next day the SPFL was 'pleased' to announce that Sky Sports had agreed to the Neo-Gers match being played at the same time as all the others, on 2nd May at 12.15pm.[7] It was as simple as that! And, since it was so simple, it immediately begs the question as to why this solution wasn't pursued in the first place. If Sky wasn't particularly bothered when the match took place then, obviously, the whole debacle was the sole responsibility of the SPFL. It looked as if a toe had been dipped in the water to test the reaction to a bit of help for Neo-Gers. Said toe was badly scalded and had to be hastily withdrawn.

Anyone that doubted that the SFA and SPFL were trying to help Neo-Gers had those doubts severely dented on the 25th April. Falkirk were winning 2-0 at Ibrox when Vuckic (who else?) scored in the 83rd minute. Full time was approaching when the board was held up indicating that there were going to be five added minutes. Nobody knew where all that injury time had come from; most of us just assumed that it was the usual 'helping hand' from the match officials. We didn't know the half of it!

The time shown on the board is not written in stone, so to speak, and the referee has discretion to add even more time if he sees fit. Euan Anderson, the referee at Ibrox that day, certainly saw fit. As one of The People themselves admitted, the match 'did go on a bit'.[8] Peter Houston, the Falkirk manager, was more damning, saying, 'It almost felt like we had to play until Rangers scored.'[9]

Posters on Twitter reckoned that a full eleven minutes of added time were played; whether or not that was true, it was definitely more than the five minutes reported. The varying times given for Nicky Law's equaliser certainly points to something fishy going on. The Neo-Gers website gives the time as 90 minutes, but does admit that there was a bit of injury time. The video on the page rather brazenly has Law scoring on the 88th minute![10] The BBC insists that the goal came before the 93rd minute,[11] while The Herald says it was in the 5th minute of injury time.[12] Confusing, isn't it?

The only thing that is certain is that there was a hell of a lot of added time that day. The Falkirk Herald, rather angrily, said, 'Nicky Law converted the equaliser and all that was left on referee Euan Anderson's watch was to kick off.'[13] It looks as if Peter Houston was

107

totally correct in his assessment of the referee's performance that day.

Neo-Gers were facing Hearts at Tynecastle the following week, the last day of the season proper, while Hibs were against Falkirk at Falkirk Stadium. Since Hibs had beaten Alloa 4-1 while Falkirk were being robbed at Ibrox, a defeat for Neo-Gers would have left them with a mountain to climb. Hibs would only have needed a draw to secure second place, with Neo-Gers having to beat Hearts by more than six goals. Euan Anderson had handed Neo-Gers a lifeline, albeit a slender one.

Meanwhile, a bit of a stooshie was taking place with Hibs challenging the 50% levy that the SPFL was going to take from ticket sales for the play-offs. The club wanted this reduced to 25%. Critics saw this as a cynical move since Hibs was definitely going to be involved in the play-offs. The fact that Motherwell supported the move seemed to justify this opinion. Hearts also being behind the Hibs proposals, however, upset this notion more than a little.

Leeann Dempster, of Hibs claimed that

> ...all the levy does is take money paid by supporters to watch the team they support and redistribute that to every other team in the league. Any club which can imagine itself in that situation would say that was unfair.[14]

There was also the little matter of season tickets, which Dempster argued should be valid for the play-off matches.[15]

It's an argument that's been going on for years; should clubs that have thousands of paying customers be subsidising wee clubs that have three old men and a dog turning up to dilapidated stadiums once a fortnight? On the other hand, should the whole game just be dominated by filthy lucre? The debate's been going on longer than some football teams have been around and will still be going on when Neo-Gers grow old.

Our media was pretty clear whose side they were on. The headlines said it all: 'Hibs bid to grab more Premiership playoff cash',[16] 'Hibernian face battle with lower league clubs over gate revenue'[17] and 'Hibernian bid to keep bigger share of Premiership play-off gate receipts'.[18] Our beloved Fourth Estate was explicit in its condemnation of the money-grubbing Hibs and their evil accomplices, Hearts and

Motherwell. It's worth bearing this viewpoint in mind and comparing it with their reaction to later developments.

This, however, was all knee-jerk stuff; nobody actually looked at the nitty-gritty of what Leeann Dempster was saying. Part of her argument was that it wouldn't be, despite what the papers were saying, the lower-league clubs that would benefit most from the levy. In fact, 82% of the money went to the clubs in the Premiership.[19] The media were being disingenuous in making out that Hibs were trying to somehow 'steal' money from deserving cases in the lower leagues.

In any case, when the matter came to a vote on the 23rd April, only Hibs, Hearts and Mothewell were in favour of the proposition. Not one other club in the whole league set-up supported them. The proposal was thrown out, meaning that the potential £1 million in revenue had been saved for distribution among the clubs.[20] Again, the note of triumph at this turn of events in our media is worth bearing in mind.

Early in April there was already a clue that our media would quickly change their mind over this issue when an article about the play-offs appeared in the Daily Record. In it the unfairness of the whole thing was pointed out as Neo-Gers was predicted to have capacity crowds if they reached the final, raising £2 million in gate money. Half of this was going to have to be handed over to the SPFL, while the prize money Neo-Gers were expected to earn for finishing second was only £342,000.[21] This obvious nod to the unfairness of the levy was quickly abandoned as the media collectively rounded on Hibs. We were, however, to encounter it again.

Meanwhile, the Neo-Gers board had a meeting with Mike Ashley, which was described as 'amicable'.[22] This was hardly credible when Murray was blaming the previous board for all the current woes of the club.[23] You could hardly see Ashley welcoming them with open arms! But, then, we had no way of knowing the truth of the situation since delisting meant that no minutes had to be sent to any pain-in-the-arse stock exchange.

Phil Mac Giolla Bhain had a different story to tell; one that was probably nearer to the truth. According to his sources, the Neo-Gers folk went to Sports Direct with cap in hand, desperate to secure some cash. The SD people gave them short shrift and sent them home with bugger all. Things were anything but amicable![24]

The lack of transparency at Ibrox was apparent again when it came to April's wage bill. Presumably everybody got their money but there was no way of knowing for certain. Our media had nothing at all to say on the matter; Level 5 no doubt couldn't find any way to put a positive spin on the situation, leaving the agnivores without a story. Once more it was Phil Mac Giolla Bhain to the rescue. Apparently, George Letham and George Taylor managed to scrounge enough to get them through, although the Ibrox gardener seemingly had to go without.[25] If he was right then things were a lot worse than anybody thought!

It has become commonplace to say that Hibs always bottle it on the big occasions. Since 1900 Hibs have been in the Scottish Cup final twelve times but have only managed to win it once, in 1902. In May 2014 they were beaten in a penalty shoot-out by Hamilton Accies to end up relegated to the second tier. And during this current season they had lost twice to Falkirk and once managed a 3-3 draw. It was entirely possible that they might blow it again.

At half-time on 2nd May Neo-Gers were winning 2-0 against Hearts at Tynecastle, while Hibs were leading by the same score-line at Falkirk Stadium. The referee had done his bit at Tynecastle in the first half, denying Hearts a stonewall penalty and hopes were no doubt running high in the Neo-Gers changing room. All it needed was for Falkirk to score two in the second half and Neo-Gers would finish second in the league and would only have to play a possible four matches in the play-offs instead of six. Things, however, didn't quite work out that way.

Hibs scored a third on the 77th minute, effectively putting the match beyond Falkirk's reach. It didn't matter now what happened at Tynecastle; Hibs had finished second. Hearts, meanwhile, were determined not to spoil their title party with a home defeat and rattled two past Bell before the end to completely ruin the day of Neo-Gers. Stuart McCall's team was now going to have to play Queen of the South in a double-header.

As early as the 29th April, even before the match against Hearts, Neo-Gers were making noises about not charging season-book holders for any of the play-off games. This was a strange U-turn; after all, they had shown no support whatsoever for Hibernian's proposal a few days earlier. They were not the only ones doing a U-turn. After all the attacks against Hibs, the media seemed to have changed their minds; there was no talk now of money-grabbing or denying vital revenue to lower-league teams. In fact, the teams in the lower leagues weren't mentioned at all.[26]

Rather brazenly, it was made out as if this was a Neo-Gers 'revolt' with Hibs and Motherwell hanging onto their coat-tails. This was Neo-Gers sticking up for their supporters in the face of a greedy SPFL. The People were, of course, overjoyed. Well, not all The People. Some saw it for what it was; a cynical attempt to get the Ashley supporters onside.

Almost from the inception of Neo-Gers, the Real Rangers Men had been trying to destroy it. Season-ticket boycotts, match boycotts, merchandise boycotts: everything was done to keep money out of Neo-Gers, ostensibly to drive 'the rats' out of the boardroom. Now the Real Rangers Men were the ones in charge and they were going to have to persuade everyone that they should buy season tickets now.

The section of The People that were in the Sons of Struth and the like, and had been waving pishy bedsheets on behalf of King and his cronies, would no doubt comply, finances permitting. But what about the ones that had turned up through thick and thin, buying season tickets since the days of Charles Green? Would the new board just take them for granted? It appeared not.

Unfortunately for the Real Rangers Men, the ones they were targeting could see right through the ploy. The website of 'Rangers Supporters Loyal' has been, from its birth, a rallying point for those that would rather have Mike Ashley running things. One commenter had this to say:

> I think you will realise brothers this being a sign of desperation for funds and purchase of forthcoming sale of season tickets.......not REALLY recognition of loyalty. Cunning boardroom members showing first glimmer of transparency to get onside but once again in my opinion the usual sleakit way.[27]

Another poster accused the board of 'using the SPFL as a tool to get in good with us long term loyal supporter after praising the boycotters but saying nothing about us'.[28]

While another called the idea of letting season-ticket holders in for free 'a misguided attempt to win the hearts and mind of a support that they fractured'.[29]

These folk might see through the manoeuvre but the agnivores in the media were prepared to back Neo-Gers to the hilt. In one of those cosy, wee chats that they show on the Daily Record website,

Keith Jackson, Tony Haggerty and Scott McDermott were all agreed that it was the fault of the SPFL.[30] Neo-Gers were quite right to be taking the stance that they were and it was even asked whether it was right that Neo-Gers should be subsidising the 'wee' clubs with the levy. This was in marked contrast to the vitriol that had been spat at Hibs only a week or so earlier.

The main point that all three men agreed on was that a precedent had been set the previous season, when Hibs had allowed their season-ticket holders in for free without punishment. This, in fact, was the whole basis of the Neo-Gers argument. It was the usual Ibrox 'whatabootery'; Hibs had got away with it, so why shouldn't Neo-Gers?

The fact was, though, that Hibs hadn't 'got away with' anything. They had actually approached the SPFL to ask if they could let season-book holders in free; they gave a valid reason and the SPFL allowed it. If any other club had asked, it would have been granted permission as well.

The reason Hibs gave in 2014, and it was a strong one, was that most of their season tickets had been sold even before the SPFL had come into being, never mind the play-off rules. The SPFL judged that Hibs had a point and allowed them to admit season-book holders into Easter Road.[31] This, however, was a one-off and for a reason that couldn't possibly occur again. It certainly wasn't a precedent.

As usual with Neo-Gers, hypocrisy was never far away. While they were arguing that season-book holders shouldn't be paying because the play-offs were part of the season, they saw nothing wrong in taking the opposite view when it suited them.

There were a couple of players in the team that were only one yellow card away from a suspension and this had Stuart McCall worried. He said, 'As soon as the season finishes, I think suspensions should be wiped out.'[32] So there we had it. On the one hand, it was to be still part of the season for season-book holders but a new, separate competition for the players so that previous yellow cards wouldn't count. And they wonder why folk don't like them?

The SPFL had no intention of backing down and the precedent argument was a non-starter so Neo-Gers had to give in. They did, however, hit on a ruse to 'get their own back', as they saw it. They were going to charge a flat rate of £5 for play-off matches at Ibrox.

That would soon teach the football authorities who was boss!

Again, the reaction to this in the media was in sharp contrast to the way Hibs had been treated. Gleefully the Daily Record announced that 'The Ibrox club stick two fingers up at the SPFL who insisted season-ticket holders had to fork out again.'[33] Note the insistence that it was unfair for season-ticket holders to have to 'fork out again'. It was obvious whose side the media were on!

The Record also added up the money involved and worked out that the revenue raised would have been more if season-ticket holders had got in for free with everyone else paying a standard amount. Whoever wrote the article also said, 'The irony also is of course that had the SPFL allowed Rangers to let season tickets count, they potentially would have made more money than they will do now.'[34] That, of course, meant less money to be distributed among the teams in the lower divisions; but nobody seemed to care about that now.

It was just like old times with the agnivores simply regurgitating everything they were fed by the Ibrox PR machine. There were Real Rangers Men in charge at Ibrox, the club was behaving however it liked with impunity and the agnivores were churning out Ibrox press releases as if they were news; all was right with the world. This was what the media, The People and the football authorities had wanted since 2012 in order to convince themselves and, hopefully, others that the Big Lie wasn't a lie at all; Rangers had never gone away.

The happiest person in all of this was, no doubt, Mr. James Sexton Traynor. He had never really been happy after he had joined Charles Green's new club; penning the odd petulant article to appear on the Neo-Gers website can hardly have been what he had been expecting. Now, here he was, in charge of Ibrox PR, standing in his offices in Blythswood Square in his chef's hat and whites dishing out the lamb dinners to the doyens of sports journalism in Scotland. He probably shed tears of happiness every night before he went to sleep.

And so May 9th arrived and Neo-Gers travelled down to Dumfries to face Queen of the South. The Ibrox club hadn't even managed to score at Palmerston that season, never mind win. This, of course, was blamed on the artificial pitch and offered the perfect excuse if Neo-Gers were to be beaten again. There was no need to worry, though. As usual, the referee was there to lend a helping hand.

Haris Vuckic might be a great player but he had also proven to be an inveterate cheat. At Palmerston he performed his usual theatrics, throwing himself to the ground if anyone so much as laid eyes on him. The referee was quite willing to give a free kick for each of these dives, so Vuckic felt justified in keeping it up. He's not averse to sticking the boot in to commit a few fouls himself; something else he gets away with a lot. No wonder he wants to stay in Scotland!

It was nearly half-time when Vuckic committed one of his by now trademark fouls just outside the Queens' goal area. Remarkably, the referee saw things differently and gave Neo-Gers a free kick. The goal scored by Stevie Smith was an absolute cracker, one that even Nakamura would have been proud of. The fact remains, though, that it shouldn't have been a free kick in the first place and Neo-Gers shouldn't have had that goal-scoring opportunity.

After QOS had equalised, the referee had to come to the rescue again. Daniel Carmichael, of QOS, was scythed down by a two-footed lunge from Ricky Foster, with studs aimed directly at Carmichael's legs. It was a straightforward red card but the referee decided otherwise and a yellow was flashed in Foster's direction. A few moments later Foster was involved in the winning goal by Dean Shiels. There was nothing wrong with the goal itself but it's debatable whether it would have occurred if Foster had been sent off and Neo-Gers reduced to ten men. It seemed, though, that this was a scenario that our football officials found it hard to countenance.

The return match, at Ibrox, would take place the following Sunday, the 17th May. With tickets only costing a fiver, Neo-Gers were hoping for a sell-out crowd. More than that; Neo-Gers decided to pack the place to the rafters with The People.

QOS were allocated only 935 tickets.[35] The Queens' manager, it has to be said, didn't seem too bothered and the club made no complaint.[36] Even if they had, the media probably wouldn't have been interested; they had a bigger story to concentrate on.

It was on the 13th May that the news hit the papers that Mike Ashley was demanding his £5m back, as he was perfectly entitled to do. Not only did he want his cash back but he wanted an EGM called so he could demand answers to questions about the delisting of Neo-Gers from the AIM and the failure to secure the services of a NOMAD.[37] This sort of news could destabilise the team, as Sooperally had once claimed, right in the middle of the most important matches in the life of the new club. What a bastard, eh?

The truth, however, was that although the story broke on the 13th

114

May, the letter from Ashley was dated the 29th April.[38] Now, folk might complain about Royal Mail but it's nowhere near as bad as that; besides, Ashley probably sent his letter by express courier. So the letter had been sitting around for two weeks before the Real Rangers Men decided to release its details to the press. This was the new era of transparency at Ibrox!

So what had prompted Ashley to suddenly descend like some vengeful god in a Greek play after weeks of inactivity? Well, that was all down to the stupidity of the Real Rangers Men. Remember those meetings that the agnivores described as amicable peace talks but which Phil Mac Giolla Bhain told us was more a case of the Real Rangers Men being snubbed by Sports Direct when they came visiting with a begging bowl? The fact that the talks came to naught would suggest that Phil's version was nearer to the truth and that things were far from amicable. Of course, the Real Rangers Men weren't used to being treated like this and, although they issued no threats themselves that we are aware of, threats were forthcoming nonetheless.

Halloween Houston, *Obergruppenführer* of the Sons of Struth, called on The People not to buy any merchandise until the 'amicable meetings' were over. He said:

> With the obvious ongoing discussions we would ask fans to consider holding off any kit purchases until the talks are concluded and we will then be in a better position to judge if the agreement is in fact a fair deal for our club.[39]

Now, this, ostensibly, was just a supporters' group giving its independent opinion. That, however, was far from true. Everybody and his mother knew that Big Jabba's Level 5 were working closely with these different groups. The website of the Union of Fans, which included the Sons of Struth in its ranks, boasted of Level 5 doing its PR work. Unfortunately, this website has now been deleted so I can't give a link.

Anyway, Ashley would have been as aware as anyone that these supporters' groups, the new board at Neo-Gers, Dave King, the Three Bears and Level 5 were all part of one, homogeneous group: the Real Rangers Men. Whatever one part said, you could be damn sure that the other parts agreed fully, like bees in a nest being directed by pheromones from the queen. This petulant threat to boycott Ashley's shops was made on the 23rd April and no doubt came straight from Jabba Central. No wonder Ashley reacted the way he did!

Even then the Real Rangers Men couldn't leave well enough alone. On the 5th May the Daily Record had a dramatic story about a police raid on Sports Direct's headquarters in Derbyshire. Apparently, uniformed officers kept everyone in the store until detectives searched the place. According to Police Scotland they were looking for documents relating to Whyte's purchase of Rangers and Green's purchase of the assets.[40]

As usual, Phil Mac Giolla Bhain had a different tale to tell. Three officers from Police Scotland turned up at Sports Direct HQ, two in plain clothes and one in uniform. They politely asked to see David Forsey, the Chief Executive, were handed two documents that they requested and left peaceably.[41] It was hardly what you would call a 'raid'.

Whatever the truth of the police visit, there are no prizes for guessing who had given the police the tip-off that said documents were in Sports Direct's possession. Whether it was an orderly visit or like something out of an American cop show, Ashley wasn't going to be too happy about the rozzers being sent to his door. This meant war!

As was always the case when it came to Neo-Gers, there was room for some comedy among all the drama. On the 12th May, the Neo-Gers website announced that six new paintings had been hung at the top of the marble staircase. These included portraits of Bill Struth, Walter Smith and Jock Wallace, but pride of place was given to one particular painting, which the Neo-Gers website described thusly:

> The new framed painting titled the New Pioneers depicts Ally McCoist, Lee McCulloch, Lee Wallace, and Neil Alexander in a mirror image of the Gallant Pioneers, Moses McNeil, Peter McNeil, William McBeath and Peter Campbell.[42]

Obviously the usual lack of sense prevailed at Ibrox. Everything about this painting was as if it were deliberately calculated to get

116

The People's backs up. It depicted a remarkably slim Sooperally, standing with his arms folded, as he had done at every match he had been in charge of, as if the dreadful display had nothing to do with him. And then there was Neil Alexander, who had had the unmitigated gall to take Neo-Gers to court to get the money he was entitled to!

Even worse, though, was the title of the painting, which the artist, Helen Runciman, had actually put on the canvas, forestalling any attempt to rename the masterpiece. There it was, in bold brush strokes, 'The New Pioneers'. Look in any dictionary and the word 'pioneer' is all about finding new places, beginning new endeavours; the key word is 'new'. This word is complete anathema to The People, for obvious reasons. And yet here it was at the top of the marble staircase! The name gave the whole game away: Sooperally and the rest were being celebrated for starting up something new. No wonder they all turned apoplectic.

The story had broken on the morning of the 12th May and it was that very afternoon that the Daily Record was able to report that the painting had been taken down.[43] Off it went to join other unwanted pieces of art, like Rolf Harris's portrait of the Queen. Meanwhile, Neo-Gers were at pains to point out that all six paintings had been ordered by Charles Green two years ago.[44] All they had done was stick them up on the wall; presumably without looking at them first!

The second leg of the game against Queen of the South proved to be something of an anti-climax. While the rest of the country hoped for and expected a QOS resurgence, The People were looking for Neo-Gers to complete the job in a convincing manner. Neither got what they wanted. The match ended in a 1-1 draw, meaning that Neo-Gers now had a possible four matches between them and the Premiership. We'd heard it before and now we were hearing it again: they were coming down the road!

14
Anarchy in the UK

The day after the defeat of QOS Keith Jackson was in the Daily Record, banging on about 'Helicopter Sundays' and Stuart McCall returning to Fir Park. Apparently, it was fate that McCall was going to emerge from Fir Park at the head of a triumphant Neo-Gers. As Jackson put it, 'It's almost as if it's been written in the stars that he will return to Fir Park in the most uncomfortable circumstances imaginable.'[1] Apparently, Hibs were an irrelevance, a fly to be swept from the windscreen as Neo-Gers progressed on 'The Journey'.

It seemed that the good folk at Neo-Gers felt exactly the same way. Even before a ball had been kicked against QOS at Ibrox, Neo-Gers let everyone know that, if they got through, they were only going to give Hibs a paltry 950 tickets. Hibs, of course, were incensed and the Hibs supporter that wrote a blog for the Daily Record, Jamie Montgomery, lost no time in making his feelings known. He said:

> It seems integrity is still low on the list of priorities at Ibrox these days, despite everything. The miserable ticket allocation for a game which is not your ordinary league encounter only proves that. If they squeeze past Queen of the South, Rangers' nerves are well and truly jangling at the thought of the mighty Edinburgh Hibees bringing the bounce to Govan.[2]

As subsequent events were to show, he wasn't far wrong.

Amazingly, or, perhaps, unsurprisingly, the day before the first leg against Hibs at Ibrox was to take place, the SFA decided that Dave King was a 'fit and proper person' to be Chairman of Neo-Gers, even though he was anything but! A statement by the SFA claimed that information had been sought from every source possible in South Africa before reaching their decision.[3]

Apparently, the SA authorities gave Honest Dave a clean bill of health. I bet they did. They'd probably do anything to try to get King and his filthy money out of their country! At any rate, King would be 'jetting in' to join The People at Ibrox the following evening.

On the same day Stuart McCall was calling on The People to get involved in the match against Hibs. He had gone on before about how he didn't like to hear boos ringing out against his team from its own supporters. Now he wanted them to act as a thirteenth man (there would be a referee there to be the twelfth!) to lift the team's spirit. He was quite candid in admitting that his team was shite and he expected The People to do their bit.[4] They certainly answered his call, and more!

Reading the BBC report on the match you would be led to believe that Neo-Gers played a magnificent game against a Hibs that had no answer to the superiority of their opponents. One little part of this report stands out: 'Allan was entitled to complain about the pieces of paper thrown at him by the home fans when he lined up to take a corner at one edge of the pitch.'[5] This incident, however, was no isolated one; it was the story of the whole match. It was left to Jamie Montgomery to set the record straight a couple of days later.[6]

The truth is that rolled-up and scrunched-up pieces of paper came raining down every time a Hibs player tried to take a corner or a throw-in. In the first half all around the Hibs goal area was practically covered in paper, every bit thrown in an attempt to hit Oxley, the Hibs goalie. The Ibrox security staff, and even the police, meanwhile, did nothing whatsoever to stop this behavior. It was as if they had been expecting it and had orders not to interfere.

The security staff and the police also stood by whenever the ball ended up in the crowd, kicked there by a Neo-Gers player. This happened too often to be a coincidence and The People refused to return the ball. It was passed from section to section before finally being flung down so that the Hibs player had to climb over the hoardings to retrieve it. The situation could have been resolved easily by the throwing onto the pitch of a spare ball, but none were in evidence; there seemed to be no ball boys available either. The Hibs players had to just stand and wait for The People to return the ball. Such circumstances only add weight to the suspicion that the whole thing had been orchestrated.

Jamie Montgomery said that it looked as if the stewards and police thought the crowd's behavior was funny[7] but anyone that watched the match wouldn't have seen much in the way of laughter. This was all deadly serious. It was calculated to put Hibs off their game and it worked a treat.

The People, as you might expect, saw things a bit differently. 'Let's get this into perspective here...some paper getting thrown and folk throwing a ball about for a minute, yes could be annoying if your wanting to get on with a game but hardly a hanging offence!'[8] What possible harm could throwing bits of paper do? seemed to be the attitude. If anyone ever throws paper at the Neo-Gers players, we'll soon be told what harm it could do; not just by The People but by all the compliant agnivores in our media.

The fact is that those pieces of paper could contain spit, blood, shit or even a bolt from the neck of one of the idiots throwing them. Players will be told to be on their guard and even their own instincts will tell them to avoid any missiles, no matter how innocuous-looking they are. The Hibs players constantly had to be dodging and shuffling about. Such things can easily put you off your game, which, in this instance, they were obviously calculated to do.

With all the stoppages, waiting for the ball, dodging paper and the like, a fair bit of injury time should have been added; of course, it wasn't. Five minutes might seem like a lot but, considering all the wasted time, double that time would still not have been enough. It wasn't just the stoppages caused by The People; the referee, Calum Murray, did his bit to stop the flow of the game as well. Not only was the whole match pretty stop-start, mostly to the benefit of Neo-Gers, but the Neo-Gers players got away with murder as well. Every time the ball was in or around the Neo-Gers goal area there was a good bit of pushing, pulling and throwing of elbows; none of which, of course, was seen by Mr. Murray. Jamie Montgomery had something to say about that.

He said that Hibs' 'passing and movement (was) frequently brought to a shuddering halt by the ever dutiful Calum Murray. The referee showed himself up to be pretty weak, constantly reacting to the Rangers crowd.'[9] Mr. Montgomery also put his finger on why the referee was so lenient and why no action was, or would be, taken against Neo-Gers for the crowd's behaviour. 'This is a club that the

SFA are moving heaven and hell to try and get back to the top tier'.[10] He'd hit the nail right on the head with that little observation!

Meanwhile, Honest Dave was confirmed at Neo-Gers, saying that he was 'deeply honoured to become the club's chairman'.[11] No doubt he was as shocked as everyone else that he had been passed 'fit and proper'! He went on to talk about restoring the club's 'values and traditions' and that he was going to 'make sure the new players who come here are capable and worthy of wearing Rangers jerseys'.[12] This was all grist to The People's mill; deliberately so since King was going to need their money.

He over-egged the pudding a bit, though, by declaring that Neo-Gers was 'a massive one, a great Club...a huge Club'. His reason for this opinion was laughable to say the least. 'One only has to look at the media interest and coverage generated by Rangers to see that,' he claims.[13] The execrable Katie Hopkins is never out of the papers so, using King's reasoning, she must be a huge celebrity rather than the sad, attention-seeking wretch we all thought she was.

King made sure that the Big Lie was well to the fore; just as Green had done and for exactly the same reason. Just as Green had relied on Sooperally, and even Walter Smith, to maintain the delusion, King and his cronies wheeled out fans' favourite John Greig. He was made Honorary Life President; it was unclear, though, whether this referred to his life or the life of the new club. Leading agnivore Roddy Forsyth confirmed that the appointment was 'designed to reassure the support that the club's traditions are secure in the hands of Dave King and his allies.'[14]

And so John Greig was able to sit in the Director's Box at Easter Road to watch the second leg between Hibs and Neo-Gers. Hibs won the game 1-0 after added time but it wasn't enough to stop Neo-Gers progressing to the final round against Motherwell. The Hibs players gave it their best shot but Neo-Gers pretty much played with the whole team in defence, making things too difficult.[15]

Of course, this being a match involving Neo-Gers, a little help from the referee had to come in somewhere. According to Alan Stubbs, the Neo-Gers players were allowed to get away with a lot of time-wasting tactics.[16] Obviously he wasn't just talking about taking the ball to the corner flag to run down the last few minutes; seemingly it went on throughout the game. The referee took no action at all to stamp it out until the seventy-fifth minute but, even then, it still went on. At the end the official time to be added on was five minutes but it should have been a lot more than that, just as it should have been at Ibrox. Hibs getting a goal in the fourth minute of injury time probably rattled the referee and he blew his whistle soon after.

The result buoyed The People no end and obviously increased the confidence of the board. In fact, the Real Rangers Men had gone off their heads and decided that they were going to take on Mike Ashley. To this end, they agreed to Ashley's demand for an EGM, which was penciled in for the 12th June. They were going to answer all his questions but were also planning to reveal all the details of the retail and marketing deal with Sports Direct. Just in case this didn't piss Ashley off enough, they had another card to play.

In their statement they spoke about the £7,500 fine that had been handed to Neo-Gers by the SFA over the breach of dual-ownership rules. Nobody seemed particularly bothered about this when it happened but, now, the Real Rangers Men had had an uncharacteristic crisis of conscience! The statement said:

> As a result of these penalties and to prevent a situation where further breaches of these rules could trigger severe sanctions on the Club, the Directors are considering incorporating (SFA) disciplinary rule 19 into the Articles of Association of the Company and disapplying voting rights in respect of any shareholding(s) which breach these rules.[17]

Obviously the bedsheet-wavers would be up for that and would be making plenty of assenting noises at the meeting. The votes of the rat catchers, however, counted for little more than bugger all; it would be down to the corporate shareholders to decide what happened. And that's where King and his pals might find that they were no longer flavour of the month. These serious shareholders would be wanting serious answers.

They might well take Ashley's side when it came to voting. After all, King had lied through his teeth about having money to plough in and about having a NOMAD lined up. All that had happened was that one set of lenders had been replaced with another, except now there was no market available to trade shares. Nobody even knew how much their shares were worth anymore. None of these

122

shareholders gave a monkey's toss about Neo-Gers, Rangers or whatever they wanted to call it. All they were interested in was making money and ensuring that they didn't lose any. It was going to be an interesting contest.

Rather incredibly, the Real Rangers Men had one more point to make in their statement; one of the resolutions they would be putting to the EGM:

> That, the shareholders support the Directors of the Company in their desire to ensure that the contractual arrangements between the Club and various members of the Sports Direct group of companies are renegotiated on a basis that is fair and reasonable for both parties and will deliver best value to both the Club and Sports Direct. The shareholders agree that these negotiations need to address the whole relationship between the Club and Sports Direct in order to achieve that goal.[18]

There was no way in Hell that Ashley would be forced to renegotiate his contracts with the club; it was going to need tact and diplomacy. Threatening to release all the details of the Sports Direct deal to make Ashley look bad as well as attempting to remove his voting rights was hardly going to entice him to the negotiating table, was it? The Real Rangers Men were playing a dangerous game.

Perhaps, though, a man had already been lined up for the job; a man of ambassadorial standing. An Ibrox legend like John Greig would surely have no trouble using his great diplomatic skills to talk Ashley round. Failing that, he could always give him a good kicking!

15
Don't Give Me No Lip, Child

It was a point already raised by Roddy Forsyth in the Telegraph; he said of the match at Easter Road that 'Rangers (were) playing their fourth game in 14 days'.[1] It was a wee shame, so it was! Of course, this idea had to be driven home with a sledgehammer by the Daily Record, which reported:

> While the Steelmen finished up on Saturday after their closing run of Premiership fixtures, Rangers have been playing two games a week, facing Queen of the South and then Hibs in the preliminary play offs.[2]

As huffy teenagers on the telly are wont to say, it was so not fair.

The Record article was about Neo-Gers defender, Ricky Foster, moaning about the unfairness of it all, under the guise of praising his teammates. 'It's a massive credit to the players inside the dressing room that we're now at this point,' he said.[3] He couldn't help adding, though, 'I think that the way that the Play-Offs are structured is not favourable to the teams that are in our division.'[4]

The fact is that the format of the play-offs was decided well in advance, with all the teams, including Neo-Gers, agreeing to it. No doubt the Ibrox club was happy enough at the start of the season, when all and sundry expected Neo-Gers to win the Championship. They were happy enough for other teams to work their way through the play-offs; it was a different story when they had to do it.

Ian Baraclough, the Motherwell manager, didn't see that his team had received, or was receiving, any great advantage. On the contrary, he was concerned about Neo-Gers gaining an advantage through the agency of their twelfth man. He said:

> There will be the need for strong refereeing by Bobby Madden and some strong decisions to be made. You hope

all that side of it is done properly, which I'm sure it will be. You just want the team that wins to have earned it.[5]

Whenever a manager draws attention to the, shall we say, 'foibles' of Scottish referees, The People always claim that this is putting undue pressure on the match official. Baraclough was, however, quite right to say what he did; especially on this occasion. Rumours abound that Bobby Madden was once a season-ticket holder at Ibrox. The rumours might well be untrue but it is noteworthy that nobody has actually denied it. Baraclough certainly seemed to think that something was amiss.

He was also, quite rightly, convinced that our football authorities didn't want Motherwell to win the play-off finals. He said:

> I get the feeling there is a big contingent of people behind Rangers. Everyone's saying they want the biggest and best teams in the Premiership and I can understand that. Television revenue is generated by big games and I understand why, from a commercial point of view, people want Rangers in the top flight. But teams have to earn the right to be there.[6]

Certainly if our agnivores in the press were to be believed, everybody connected with Scottish football was desperate for Neo-Gers to be in the top tier. Not that they were favouring one team, you understand; it was all for the good of the game in Scotland.

The Motherwell supporters didn't hold out much hope of a victory for their team. The Fir Park club had an absolutely shameful record against the old Rangers, prompting suspicions and claims that they were actually losing deliberately. Even in their one encounter with Neo-Gers, in the League Cup in September 2012, Motherwell fans had to face the embarrassment of seeing their team beaten 2-0 by a Third Division club. The nagging doubts about their team's potential performance against Neo-Gers showed through in the online comments of the Motherwell supporters.[7]

> Baraclough will now go baws out 4-4-2 with two wide men, and we'll get absolutely slaughtered.

> Can't imagine a single scenario where we win this.

125

I don't trust us to put men behind the ball competently for 90 minutes at Ibrox either tbf.

I can't see us doing anything other than rolling over and getting our bellies tickled like we do every single time we set eyes on a Rangers jersey and I expect the tie to be all over after next week's game at Ibrox as our side just does not possess the character and guts to go there and get anything and I can see us losing by at least three goals.

Will Partick become our new rivals when the well open their arses to Rangers?

The People, on the other hand, were bullish about their chances; their team was going to beat Motherwell convincingly.[8]

I believe we will have the most desire to win. And win we shall!!!!! For we are the Famous Glasgow Rangers.
I reckon our guys will torture their defence, McManus especially, who Jig would beat in a foot race...confident...
they've been shite all season, and we've got momentum.....can see a Vuckic pearler followed by a Clark tap in.....2-0 will be enough.

I reckon it will finish 4-1 with Law, Vukic, Miller & Boyd getting on the score sheet!

3 nil a walk in the park.

Our esteemed Fourth Estate, meanwhile, was more concerned with ticket allocations; more specifically, the 1500 tickets allocated to Neo-Gers for the second leg at Fir Park.[9] While the Daily Record ranted against this 'paltry' amount, Stuart McCall was, apparently, worried about trouble. He said, 'I have no doubt that there will be Rangers supporters elsewhere in the ground and if there are I hope nothing kicks off.'[10]

This wasn't going to happen at all since Motherwell had already taken the expedient of only selling to 'season-ticket holders, Well Society members or Well fans who are on the club's database and have purchased home end tickets before'.[11] So, unless there were Neo-Gers supporters that had been pretending to be Motherwell fans for years, McCall's projected scenario was unlikely to come to pass.

126

McCall wasn't finished having a dig at Motherwell, though. He said that it 'will be the last game in British football this season on Sunday and I'm sure there will be a big audience. It will look poor when the camera pans in behind one goal and there are empty seats.'[12]

This was all part-and-parcel of the way our game was being viewed by the Scottish media these days. Ever since Rangers died in 2012 and Neo-Gers rose to take their place, all that was important was money. Neo-Gers needed to be in the top tier to generate more income; Celtic was losing money hand-over-fist without 'Rangers'; nobody wanted to sponsor a league with no 'Rangers' in the top division; television companies didn't want to fork out for a 'Rangersless' Premiership. Nothing else mattered. Sportsmanship, excitement, die-hard support; none of that appealed to the agnivores. All they seemed to be interested in was filthy lucre.

Of course, all this concern about cold, hard cash, or the lack of it, had never been expressed much prior to the demise of Rangers. It was all a smokescreen for the desperate desire of our media to see Neo-Gers 'back where they belong'. They all knew full well that anyone watching on television wanted to see an exciting, eventful match; they wouldn't be even remotely interested in counting empty seats!

The fact was that, despite all the wailing and gnashing of teeth in the Scottish media, the whole situation had been of Neo-Gers' making. It seems that an agreement had already been reached between the two clubs, whereby Motherwell would receive 2000 tickets for Ibrox and Neo-Gers would get the whole South Stand at Fir Park, which holds 4800. As soon as the match at Easter Road was over, however, and Neo-Gers were through to the final, they reneged on the deal and sold most of the tickets to their own supporters, leaving Motherwell with just 950. Of course, just like Hibs, the Fir Park club retaliated and restricted Neo-Gers to just 1500 tickets.[13] Nobody could blame Motherwell for acting the way they did; nobody, that is, except the agnivores in the Scottish media.

When it came to the match at Ibrox on the 28th May somebody forgot to give Motherwell a copy of the script. Instead of playing to a rigid formation, Baraclough's team was flexible and moved with a fluidity that Neo-Gers completely lacked. They defended ferociously and attacked on the break with a turn of speed that

127

made Neo-Gers look like a team of Subbuteo players.

In desperation McCall threw on Kris Boyd, Tom Walsh and Shane Ferguson but it was to no real avail. Yes, they managed to pull a goal back but it was too little, too late. The People looked on in shock; this wasn't supposed to have happened! Their team had been shown up for the pile of shite that it was.

The agnivores praised Tom Walsh to the heavens, claiming that he'd made a huge difference and was Neo-Gers' best player. That, however, wasn't saying very much. They could have thrown a tailor's dummy in a blue jersey onto the pitch and it would have been better than all the Neo-Gers players around it! Not that the agnivores could bring themselves to admit that.

The best bit of the whole match happened on the sidelines rather than on the pitch. It was Stuart McCall scrambling about in the Motherwell technical area to retrieve the ball for a throw-in.[14] He was desperate to get the ball back into play; a marked contrast to all the time-wasting tactics employed in both of the matches against Hibs!

According to McCall, 'too many of us had off nights' and they were going to 'play a different way on Sunday'.[15] Everyone in our media spoke of Neo-Gers having a 'lifeline' in that one goal they scored at Ibrox. This was all they had to cling to. The Daily Record's live coverage showed how desperate they were. The excitement was palpable when McGregor scored and Gregor Kyle typed, 'GOAL! GOAL RANGERS!!!'[16]

When Hibs took a two-goal deficit to Easter Road it was claimed in the papers that they had a mountain to climb. This time round, it seemed, a two-goal deficit wasn't so insurmountable. Neo-Gers could still do it; that game at Ibrox had been a one-off, both in terms of how good Motherwell had been and how badly Neo-Gers played. Surely the Ibrox club could turn things around!

The desperation of the agnivores bordered on the risible; for example, this headline in the Daily Record:

Kris Boyd set for Rangers S.O.S call as Stuart McCall looks to rescue tie against Motherwell.[17]

The article made the rather ridiculous claim that

128

Boyd, who has barely featured since McCall took over from Kenny McDowall in March, posed Well problems when he came off the bench in the first leg of the Premiership play-off final on Thursday.[18]

They must have been watching a different match from the rest of us. In reality all Boyd managed was one lucky shot on goal and then, later, falling on his arse and trying to claim a penalty. Baraclough's men must have been shiting themselves!

The 31st was soon upon us and, as the press hadn't tired of telling us, the first goal was going to be important. The hope seemed to be that Neo-Gers would score early and frighten Motherwell into submission. It didn't quite happen that way; in fact, the first half turned out to be pretty boring. Neo-Gers huffed and puffed but achieved nothing, while the referee decided not to adhere to the normal SFA rulebook. Vuckic was booked for one of his now customary dives and Miller's claims for a penalty were waved away derisively.

The only real entertainment was provided by a silly, old bugger, who decided to use the large flag he was carrying to flick the ball to Lee McCulloch when he was going to take a throw-in. The old fool mistimed his flick and ended up hitting McCulloch in the face! As McCulloch threw his hands to his face theatrically, the old guy said his apologies and gave the player a soft, kid-on skelp on the buttock with the flagpole to emphasise his contrition. Maybe McCulloch wouldn't be so free with his elbows in future, now that he knew what it was like to be on the receiving end!

The Daily Record's ace reporter, Gregor Kyle, decided to use the incident for a quick bit of sucking up to The People. He said:

As much as some are making light of this, you can actually see the guilty party have a second swing at McCulloch and catch him on the backside. In recent years I've seen people banned from grounds and stopped by the cops at airports for less (true story).[19]

Anyone that actually saw what happened knew this was a load of shite.

The second half was only a few minutes old when Motherwell scored. A Marvin Johnson shot took a deflection off Zaliukas's leg and headed for the top corner of the Neo-Gers goal. Cammy Bell saw it coming

129

from a mile off but, instead of dealing with it he backed towards the goalmouth and flapped at the ball with his hand like a big Jessie. Needless to say, the ball ended up in the back of the net.

After that Neo-Gers went back to their default tactic of punting hopeful balls up the pitch. Motherwell, on the other hand, reverted to the flexible positioning that had proven so effective in the last match. The goal had settled Baraclough's team and now there seemed little doubt as to who the winner was going to be.

A cracker of a goal from Ainsworth, again built up on the break, put things beyond Neo-Gers and The People started to head for the exits. A few minutes later McCall inexplicably replaced Zaliukas with the walking disaster zone that was Bilel Mohsni. Everybody watching shook their heads in disbelief; what the hell was the point?

John Sutton came on as a substitute in the dying moments; just in time to take the penalty resulting from Lee Erwin being tripped in the box. Of course, there was no way he was going to miss and Motherwell ended the match as 3-0 winners; 6-1 overall. Neo-Gers were going to have to spend another year in the Championship.

The match, unfortunately, ended in violence; not among the fans but among the players. Lee Erwin offered his hand for Bilel Mohsni to shake, only to be rebuffed. According to Erwin, Mohsni not only refused to shake his hand but told him to 'Fuck off!' Erwin gave Mohsni a sharp push and the Tunisian responded with a kick and then a punch to Erwin's face, drawing blood in the process. Other players got involved and it was almost a mass brawl before saner teammates pulled them all apart.[20]

It's debatable which is the more shameful: this behaviour by professional players or the desperate attempts by our media to cast the Motherwell supporters in a bad light. Reports that 'supporters ran on the pitch and taunted the Rangers supporters'[21] and that 'Motherwell fans rushed to challenge the travelling Rangers fans'[22] suggested that the Motherwell fans were nothing more than a gang of troublemaking thugs.

The truth is that Motherwell fans always run onto the pitch at the end of the last home game of the season; they've been doing it for years. This time was no different, with the added bonus that there was actually something to celebrate.

Probably the most disgusting article attacking the Motherwell supporters was penned by David McCarthy in the Daily Record;

where else? According to McCarthy, hundreds of Motherwell supporters ran onto the pitch and made straight for the 'away' section to taunt and goad the 1500 Neo-Gers fans.[23] It seems that standards have dropped so much at the Daily Record that, as well as a decent grasp of the English language no longer being a prerequisite for employment as a journalist, basic maths is not required. Even the most cursory of glances at the picture accompanying McCarthy's article shows that the numbers of Motherwell fans on the pitch barely reaches treble figures. Equally, most of the Neo-Gers supporters had sneaked out the exits ages before and there were less than a hundred left.

Four mounted policemen cleared the pitch in a matter of minutes, which hardly squares with McCarthy's version of events. A quartet of cops on cuddies would hardly manage against the hundreds of
bloodthirsty savages that McCarthy tries to make us envisage.
Furthermore, the speed with which the mounted policemen turned up proves that they were already on standby. The Motherwell fans aren't renowned for causing trouble so there's only one reason why that horseflesh was around in the first place. The reputation of The People precedes them wherever they go.

There's a video on YouTube, captured from Sky TV, which shows the crowd of Motherwell fans jumping about, hands in the air, celebrating.[24] There are, granted, one or two idiots over at the Neo-Gers section, laughing at The People and even, you could argue, goading them. It's hardly the scene, however, that McCarthy describes. Nor was it in any way comparable to the 1980 Scottish Cup final, as the Daily Record insisted.[25]

Why our media should decide to exaggerate the seriousness of the Mothewell pitch invasion is unclear. While they complained that it didn't reflect well on Scottish football they seemed hell-bent on making sure that it remained in the public eye; and nobody actually thought it was that bad until they made it appear so. It certainly wasn't going to make The People feel any better; their team had been well beaten no matter what. Perhaps the agnivores held out a faint hope that, somehow, if they kept on about it for long enough, Motherwell might be disqualified and Neo-Gers given their place in the Premiership!

131

As for Bilel Mohsni, he was absolved of any blame and the guilt laid squarely at Lee Erwin's door. This, however didn't come from any football authority. It came from a far more important one; Mohsni's mammy.[26] Meanwhile a letter made its way from Hampden to Bolton, informing Neil Lennon that if he ever returned to Scottish football he faced an immediate six-game suspension.

<u>16</u>
<u>No One Is Innocent</u>

W e looked earlier at the continued insistence by The People that there had been some dodgy deals between Glasgow City Council and Celtic FC, to the huge benefit of the latter. The wee, sad man in Belfast, who called himself PZJ, was still beavering away on his pointless quest, while the Derry Dinosaur Jockey, Gregory Campbell, desperately awaited new questions about Celtic that he could raise in Westminster. Bill McMurdo and his followers in Rangers Supporters Loyal were firm adherents of all this nonsense about corruption in Glasgow City Chambers. They decided, however, to add a new dimension; one that most of The People would find hard to swallow.

It was mostly in the 'Comments' section of the Rangers Supporters Loyal blog that the new suspicions were voiced. It wasn't, however, just the rank and file that were coming up with these notions; McMurdo himself was a believer and one guy claimed to have dug deep and discovered all manner of evidence.[1] The story was that King and his cronies were planning to sell Ibrox, Auchenhowie and the rest. Apparently, Glasgow Council was planning massive redevelopment and the area around Ibrox Stadium was going to be worth a fortune. Neo-Gers, meanwhile, would move to some new, purpose-built stadium.

And that wasn't the worst of it. The media had been running anti-Ashley stories for ages; obviously fed them by Jabba's company, Level 5. According to Rangers Supporters Loyal, Level 5 was some kind of Masonic reference, to do with resurrection. We mere mortals aren't particularly au fait with Great Architects, Widows' Sons, pressing the correct knuckle and the like; so we'll have to take their word for it. Resurrection – new team, new home and the rest – get it? As one of them put it, 'Rangers fans – we are being let down by our own.'[2]

As mad as this theory sounds it might well have been the truth; there was no way of knowing. Perversely, given how much the Real

Rangers Men and the bedsheet-wavers had gone on about 'transparency', it was now harder to discern what was going on at Ibrox than it had been under Ashley's regime. Neo-Gers might still be billed as a 'PLC' but, to all intents and purposes, it was now a private company.

The agnivores in our media were happy enough; the good old days of succulent-lamb-scented press releases were back! The Daily Record appeared to be the organ of choice as far as Level 5 was concerned; it was as if Jabba had never been away. A lot of The People were content with all this spoon-fed guff. McMurdo's mob, on the other hand, were far from chuffed; hence their suspicions that all was not well.

The Real Rangers Men had already threatened to reveal all the details of the Sports Direct deal at the EGM and, just to whet everybody's appetite, the Daily Record was able to print some shocking news. It seemed that Ashley's hold on the retail side of Neo-Gers was tighter than anyone had thought. If the club wanted to end the relationship, it had to give SEVEN YEARS' notice.[3] So, rather than the deal being set for a certain time frame, as everyone had thought, Ashley actually had a revolving contract.

Of course, The People, with the exception of McMurdo's Mob, were livid. The Rangers Supporters Loyal, though, could hardly spin things as being great for their club so, in a sense, they were just as angry as the rest of the Neo-Gers support. The angriest of all, however, had to be Ashley. He's never been one to do his dealings out in the open and wouldn't appreciate this revelation. As on other occasions, he kept his own counsel and said nothing.

This piece of information showed the dilemma facing The People. Yes, Ashley was a billionaire and that was what The People desperately wanted at Ibrox. The only problem was that he was obviously out to make money for his own company and, ultimately, himself; he didn't seem to particularly care about Neo-Gers. The Real Rangers Men, on the other hand, professed to care deeply about the club but they had nowhere near the financial resources that Ashley had. In fact, they were talking about it going to take years for Neo-Gers to be anywhere near to being able to challenge Celtic. This was hardly what The People wanted to hear.

The best case scenario would be if King and Ashley could work together; that boat, however, had long since sailed. The underhand way that the Real Rangers Men had gone about things: instigating season-ticket boycotts, encouraging boycotts of official retail outlets and bad-mouthing Ashley in the media, was not exactly calculated to endear them to Ashley, either in a business sense or in a personal capacity. They had pretty much worked to destroy Neo-Gers and had helped to drive the share price down.

The only thing that King and his cronies had to recommend them was that they were Real Rangers Men, which helped to strengthen the Big Lie and perpetuate the myth that the club playing out of Ibrox was 'still Rangers'. This was the only attraction of the new board and it was a pretty precarious way of getting and maintaining support.

And so the split within The People intensified. The fact that both Ashley and the Real Rangers Men preferred to work in secret, keeping everyone else in the dark, fed the paranoia of both sides of the argument. In truth, there wasn't a lot to choose between Ashley and King; neither was famed for his philanthropy and both seemed to favour the business model of providing loans to the club. To outsiders the balance tipped slightly towards Ashley, since he wasn't a convicted crook. But, then, he wasn't a 'Real Rangers Man' and that counted for more as far as most of The People, and the agnivores in our media were concerned.

The only thing that they could all agree on was the Big Lie itself. They constantly went on about how all and sundry had claimed that their club was 'still Rangers'; UEFA, the Advertising Standards Authority, the European Clubs Association etc. It was, however, a pile of crap; they knew it and we knew it. Nobody outside of Scotland had actually come out and said any such thing. That was why they pounced on anything that looked like it was supporting the Big Lie.

On the 24th May the Daily Record provided them with what looked like the ultimate in supporting arguments for the Big Lie. The opening salvo in the article said it all: 'Despite claims that Rangers are a new club, FIFA have stepped into the argument and insisted that Rangers are the same football club.'[4] Well, you couldn't get much higher an authority than FIFA, could you? We could now look forward to numerous assertions by The People that it had been proven beyond all doubt; the club they followed was 'still Rangers' and that was official!

Other newspapers ran the same story, desperate to show that the Big Lie wasn't a lie after all. The quote given by all the papers was, 'After their enforced relegation in 2012, Glasgow Rangers are in the hunt for promotion back to Scotland's top flight.'[5] It wasn't an outright, categorical statement but it was pretty conclusive nonetheless.

The problem was, however, that the quote was from the front of FIFA's weekly magazine, promoting an article within, entitled 'Rangers eye top-flight return'. This article was written by a Swedish writer, Peter Eggenberger, about whom it's difficult to find any information. There is a Wikipedia article on him; but it's in Swedish. My knowledge of Swedish only extends to being able to order a cup of coffee (a useless skill, since I don't like coffee) but I'll provide the link in case any polyglot out there can manage.[6]

Our agnivores were desperate to show that since FIFA's magazine was advertising the article the way it was, then FIFA must agree with what the article was saying. That, of course, is utter garbage. Selina Scott, the one-time newsreader, used to write a page every week in the Daily Record's sister paper, the Sunday Mail. Most weeks Scott's pieces were a load of right-wing, Tory crap, reflecting her own views, which certainly weren't those of the Daily Record and Sunday Mail. That, however, didn't stop them advertising Scott's ramblings on their front page. Equally, the advertising of Eggenberger's article in FIFA's magazine didn't necessarily mean that FIFA endorsed the content of the article. All in all it was a rather feeble argument by our media.

The fact that an argument might be feeble, however, has never stopped The People from utilising it. This time, though, they desisted from claiming that FIFA was on their side almost immediately. This wasn't from any realisation of how specious the argument was; it was for other reasons entirely.

It was only a couple of days after the nonsense about the FIFA magazine that FBI agents raided the headquarters of CONCACAF (Confederation of North, Central America and Caribbean Association Football) and the Swiss police arrested FIFA officials at their hotel in Zurich. Meanwhile U.S. Attorney General, Loretta Lynch, said, 'They (FIFA) corrupted the business of worldwide soccer to serve their interests and to enrich themselves.'[7] With all this going on it was hardly a time to align yourself with FIFA or to claim that the organisation was 'on your side'!

The Sons of Struth looked on enviously at the crisp, clean, linen bedsheets that were employed to shield the arrested men from the public gaze and were bitterly disappointed, like the rest of The People, that such a thing had to happen now of all times. Just when they were ready to smugly gloat about FIFA confirming that their club was 'still Rangers' the bastards had to go and get themselves banged up!

To borrow a phrase from renowned historian AJP Taylor, a few officials would probably be thrown to the wolves while it was quietly assumed that the rest of the footballing world had 'been somewhere else at the time'. The American Attorney General, however, had stated that all the corruption was 'deep-rooted'.[8] Football associations around the world, therefore, weren't taking any chances. There were reports of earth tremors everywhere but they weren't caused by shifting tectonic plates or by fracking operations; they were due to the frantic vibrations of the thousands of overworked shredding machines.

And what of our own football association; the SFA? From the days when Jim Farry stalked the corridors at Park Gardens to the desperate attempts to cover up for Dougie McDonald, most folk have suspected that not everything is kosher in the Scottish Football Association. Nowadays those suspicions centre on just three letters: E, B and T.

Campbell Ogilvie, the president of the SFA, received a 'loan' through David Murray's dodgy scheme to the tune of £95,000; a fact that casts serious doubt on his suitability for the job. As early as September 2011 questions were being raised about Rangers being granted a licence to play in Europe when they owed money to HMRC.[9] Ogilvie was vice-president and then president during the time that the licence was granted; should he have been in such a position when he was financially beholden to one Scottish football club?

There were calls for his resignation in 2012 when Rangers died and Neo-Gers were touted as 'the same club'. It was a serious concern that no investigations could be seen to be neutral while Ogilvie and his EBT were in charge.[10] The subsequent Nimmo-Smith inquiry, with SFA officials blatantly misrepresenting their own rules, showed that football supporters had been right to be concerned. Still Ogilvie clung to power and nobody made any attempt to shift him.

In 2014 Ogilvie threw his hat into the ring for election as Vice-President of FIFA.[11] As things turned out he lost to the English FA's David Gill; an outcome that he's probably now viewing with relief.

137

As David Gill and everyone else tries to put as much distance between themselves and Sepp Blatter, Ogilvie can shake his head and tut-tut from the sidelines.

In June 2015 Ogilvie was replaced as SFA President by Alan McRae[12] and so ended Mr. EBT's reign at the top of Scottish football. Where was he off to now? Earlier in the year Ogilvie had tried, and failed, to get himself elected onto the UEFA Executive Committee. In fact, he came second-bottom in both rounds of voting.[13] A man like Ogilvie, however, probably already had something lined up; possibly some kind of post at Level 5 awaited.

As the media reported on the end of Ogilvie's tenure, they indulged in a little recap of his time in office. Obviously they wanted to keep things positive; unfortunately, there wasn't very much positive that they could say. The best they could manage was:

> He replaced George Peat as SFA president in 2011 before presiding over the re-organisation of Scotland's league set-up in 2013.
> The Scottish Football League and Scottish Premier League merged to form the Scottish Professional Football League.
> A play-off system was introduced for the top-flight, while a pyramid set-up handed Highland League clubs and teams from the newly-formed Lowland League an opportunity to play their way into the senior ranks.[14]

Not much of a legacy, was it? It was left to an 'Internet Bampot' to detail Ogilvie's real legacy. Lies, cheating, bias and a neck that has to be cleaned with Duraglit are catalogued as being all part-and-parcel of the Ogilvie regime.[15] Yes; a job involving our media would suit him down to the ground!

17
C'Mon Everybody

I t was that time of year again, when teams try to get everybody to buy season books, promising that the coming season was going to be the best yet. It was going to be difficult for Neo-Gers to make any such promises since they faced another year in the Championship. The club, and Level 5, of course, were, however, going to give it their best shot.

Publicity shots were sent out to the press featuring King, who had 'jetted' back in for the occasion, at Ibrox, surrounded by people of different ages. 'For Generations,' said the large piece of card he held in his hands. This was the theme of the publicity for the Neo-Gers season-ticket sale. It was a direct appeal to The People, extending the Big Lie to say that not only had 'Rangers' been around for a hundred and forty-odd years, but that it would be around for a long time yet. It was quite a clever concept; buy your ticket to continue the dreams of generations past, while ensuring that the club goes on 'for generations' yet to come. I never knew Big Jabba had it in him!

Unfortunately, the Real Rangers Men seemed to have quite unrealistic expectations for the uptake of season books. King was looking to shift 45,000 season tickets; that was more than the biggest attendance at Ibrox during the previous season! King tried to rouse The People to the task by asking them 'to think back to three seasons ago when, for their first home game in the Third Division, Rangers had the biggest attendance in the UK.'[1] He seemed to have forgotten the fact that this huge crowd was down to a combination of bloody-minded defiance by The People and the cheapness of the tickets!

The average home attendance in season 2012-2013 was 45,744,[2] the kind of crowd that had rarely been seen at Ibrox in subsequent seasons. Again, though, this was in large part due to the cheapness of both tickets and season books. In fact, many supporters used a glitch in the system to wangle themselves half-price juvenile season tickets. Not for nothing are The People renowned for having short arms and deep pockets! And yet King was expecting them to fork out for a repeat leg of 'The Journey' at an increased price.

The appeal for 45,000 diehard fans/mugs to fork out for season tickets also had the undesired effect of making it look as if the Real Rangers Men were skint. King sounded desperate, saying, 'We would have to move 45,000 season tickets to reach a target of between £12m and £13m,' and 'It is a combination of the fans' support and increased funding that we require over the next three years'.[3] It seemed suspiciously like the Real Rangers Men wanted The People to bankroll their regime.

King then went on to confirm the assessment that a South African judge had made about him. 'So far, since we came in, we have demonstrated that we have done everything we said we were going to do,' he claimed.[4] Really? The Real Rangers Men and their cheerleaders had shouted non-stop about transparency and, yet, the board's dealings were now about as transparent as a stagnant pool on a dark night. And what about the promised fan representation on the board? There had been no replacement at all for the disgraced Listy Graham. Then there was the promised new NOMAD, among other things.

He went on, 'The club needed money – we put the money in. That's an absolute fact.'[5] As the wee neds used to say on Chewing The Fat, 'Naw it isnae!' Exactly what money they'd put in he omitted to mention. They'd bought their shares from other shareholders, so no money went into the club in that way. And when the club needed money for the wage bill they had loaned the cash, exactly the way that the Easdales and Mike Ashley had done. The only difference was that nobody knew what the terms of the Real Rangers Mens' loans were. It was doubtful that they'd been as philanthropic as the Easdales had been!

King rounded off his sales pitch by saying, 'We've done our bit'.[6] In other words, it was time for the supporters to dig deep into those pockets. To reinforce his message, he sent a letter out to all the current season-ticket holders; the very ones that, only a matter of months before, the bedsheet-wavers had derided as 'traitors' for not buying into King's boycott. He continued the theme of 'For Generations' by saying:

Like all of you who read this letter, I have always taken pride in being a Rangers supporter. It is something I inherited from my

140

father who, in turn, inherited the legacy from my grandfather.[7]

There goes that 'glib and shameless' stuff again. This wasn't what he had told everybody before. Only a year previously, he had told, in a newspaper interview, how

> My father wasn't at all keen on me becoming a Rangers supporter. He was a Glasgow policeman and because of that he resented the whole football scene in Glasgow. He was actually very anti-football.[8]

So much for those 'generations,' eh?

The rest of this particular article shows that it's not only about football and business that King lies; his whole life appears to be one, big fabrication. Supposedly, he and his family moved to Castlemilk when it was first built. He said:

> I don't think we ever regarded ourselves as well off in any way. You understand when you are a kid that a lot of kids are better off than you. That becomes a motivation in a way…there was a certain sense of growing up and thinking "I don't want my kids to live like this."[9]

To most of us that moved to Castlemilk in the 50s and 60s, from the Gorbals and other inner-city areas, our new home was a paradise. Your own lavvy, not shared with your next-door neighbours, a real bath with taps on it, space, light, a garden to play in and a real farm at the top of the street. It was a great place to grow up. It makes you wonder if King actually ever lived there at all! It's a bit like all the shite about Sean Connery growing up in a slum tenement in Edinburgh's Fountainbridge and yet, for some reason, going to primary school in the posh Sciennes area.

Anyway, I digress. He went on in his letter:

> We have to spend immediately to rebuild the football staff at all levels but we can't say for certain how much it will cost to forge a team to win the Championship. What I can say, however, is that if I, and other investors have to put

in an extra £5m for this season that's what we'll do. If it requires more, for instance £10m, so be it.[10]

The operative word there is 'if'; it was obvious that the Real Rangers Men were hoping that those 'ifs' didn't happen.

Right in the middle of all these begging letters and promises to, maybe, spend fortunes, came a massive bolt from the blue, if you'll pardon the pun. Ashley had woken up and decided to do something about those pesky scoundrels on the new Ibrox board. So they were going to reveal all the details of his retail deal with Neo-Gers, were they? He'd soon put a stop to that!

On 11th of June, the day before the EGM, Mike Ashley secured an injunction at the High Court in London, stopping any discussion of his contracts with Neo-Gers at the meeting.[11] He even went to the trouble of applying for an interdict at the Court of Session in Edinburgh,[12] just to make sure. King's plan to try to turn the tables on Ashley at the EGM wasn't going to happen.

The EGM itself turned out to be a complete anti-climax and a monumental waste of time. Ashley didn't bother turning up and he didn't send any representatives either, which makes you wonder why he bothered to call the meeting in the first place! It was certainly a great disappointment for the Sons of Struth and their fellow-travelers; they had probably been up all night getting those bedsheets ready. Instead, the whole thing just ended up being a cheerleading session for the Real Rangers Men.

Strangely, King didn't appear either. He was reported as being at a meeting in London; probably busy getting all those institutional investors on board. Still, when the votes were counted up a couple of days later his resolutions, unsurprisingly, had won. Neo-Gers wouldn't be paying Ashley back anytime soon and, apparently, they would be looking to renegotiate the contracts with Sports Direct. Presumably they wouldn't try to piss Ashley off any more than they already had before trying to get him to the negotiating table.

One more item came up at the EGM; one that showed the intellectual capacity of The People for what it was. Halloween Houston and his cronies called for a boycott of all official Neo-Gers merchandise; they were going to hit Ashley where it hurt. Unfortunately, this call failed to recognise the fact that Ashley wouldn't lose out on a penny if such a boycott went ahead. One of the terms of Sports Direct's contract with Neo-Gers was that the club had to pay for all unsold replica shirts and other merchandise. All they were going to achieve was to cost their club money that it couldn't afford.

As if that weren't bad enough, Phil Mac Giolla Bhain had disastrous news for The People. It appeared that Honest Dave was in London on the 12th June looking for money after all. The problem was that it wasn't institutional investors he was seeing; it was, of all folk, Mike Ashley! It seems that King was there with the begging bowl, asking for the other £5million of Ashley's promised £10million loan, beseeching Ashley not to exercise his security over the Neo-Gers assets and entreating him to lend the Ibrox club more players from NUFC. The most damning revelation, however, was that King had actually offered to sell Ashley his shares.[13] It looked as if Honest Dave wanted to get the hell out of Dodge.

Of course, this led to abuse from The People, some of which showed up on Phil's blog since he seemed to have abandoned his usual moderation procedures. Other sections of the Neo-Gers support, however, decided against shooting the messenger. Amazingly, on the 'Rangers Supporters Loyal' blog, among all the usual moans, groans and Catholic bashing in the comments section, credibility was given to the story.[14] It seemed their distrust of King outweighed their hatred of Phil Mac Giolla Bhain.

As he quite often does, Phil challenged anyone connected with Neo-Gers to contradict his story. As usual, nobody did. But, then, Level 5 had a more important job at hand. Neo-Gers had found a new manager, somebody none of us had ever heard of before, called Mark Warburton. Of course, none of us had heard of Ronny Deila either before Celtic appointed him, but at least he had a proven record of winning cups and titles. Warburton, on the other hand, was an unknown quantity. Yes, he had led Brentford from Division 1 to the Championship but that was it. Most of his success had come on the floor of the Stock Exchange rather than on the football field. Maybe King was hoping for a few tips on the financial side.

The appointment of Warburton inevitably led to a flood of

bread-related jokes. But let's not repeat any of that here; it was plain that the new manager was going to struggle so there was no need to pan him. Besides, the Ibrox saga has been joke enough in itself without adding any more attempts at comedy. Anyway, the attempts by our agnivores, led by Level 5, to make Warburton seem on a par with Alex Ferguson or Jock Stein were more hilarious than any bread jokes.

The Daily Record, Level 5's propaganda sheet of choice, led the cheerleading, saying that Warburton had 'taken (Brentford) to the brink of the English Premier League.'[15] In fact, Brentford had finished fifth in the Championship and then were knocked out of the play-offs by Middlesbrough. It looks good when you read how Brentford were beaten in the semi-finals, until you realise that there were only four teams involved in the play-offs. Warburton's team, then, only played two games and lost both.

The play-offs in the English Championship pretty much confirmed the league placings; fourth-placed Middlesbrough beat fifth-placed Brentford, third-placed Norwich beat sixth-placed Ipswich and then Norwich beat Middlesbrough in the final. Looked at from this perspective, Brentford can hardly be said to have been on the 'brink of the Premiership'.

Contrast this with Stuart McCall's record with Neo-Gers. His team finished third in the Scottish Championship, beat the fourth-placed and the second-placed teams in the play-offs and only failed at the last hurdle, against superior, Premiership, opposition. By any neutral reckoning, McCall's play-off record is a lot better than Warburton's!

The knee-jerk response is that Warburton's team was playing in the English Championship, against better teams than Hibs and Queen of the South; this, however, is nonsense. It was like against like; Brentford was an English Championship team as well, while McCall's team had to play against a club from the league above.

And, yet, McCall was being portrayed as a failure, Warburton as the best hing since…well…sliced bread. As Jimmy Greaves used to say, football's a funny old game; it certainly is in the Scottish media.

As the good book says, by their signings shall ye judge them, so everyone, especially the agnivores, waited with bated breath to see what Warburton's new team was going to look like. One thing seemed certain; it couldn't be any worse than Sooperally's Army!

The first official signing turned out to be Danny Wilson, the erstwhile Hearts captain. When questioned about abandoning the newly-promoted, and extremely promising, Hearts team for at least another year in the Championship, Wilson acted like a petulant child. He said, 'I don't need to justify my decision to anybody. It's my decision, it's my life. I'm quite happy with the decision I've made and hopefully I can be part of successful times here.'[16]

Online rumours pointed to the real reason why Wilson had signed up to Neo-Gers; he was apparently going to get £8000 a week.[17] It looked as if Sooperally's tactic of signing highly-paid mercenaries was continuing. That salary of Wilson's, moreover, works out at over £400,000 a year. That's not as much as a gardener gets paid at Ibrox but it would still need the sale of about 1000 season tickets to cover it.

It was only a matter of hours before the next signing was announced. It was a youngster called Rob Kiernan from the mighty Wigan Athletic. Kiernan is only twenty-four but has already been around a bit, appearing for Watford, Kilmarnock, Yeovil Town, Bradford City, Wycombe Wanderers, Accrington Stanley, Burton Albion, Brentford, Southend United and Birmingham City. For those that can't be bothered counting, that makes Neo-Gers his twelfth club. That's an average of two clubs a year since he first turned out for the senior squad at Watford in 2009.

As if that weren't bad enough, he's suffered ankle ligament and hamstring injuries in the past couple of years. In fact, he was meant to be signing for Birmingham City, where he had been on loan, but he seemingly failed the medical.[18] No details were given but Birmingham decided that they weren't going to take a chance.

Of course, nobody at Neo-Gers wanted to admit that they'd signed a no-hoper so Kiernan himself spoke out. The words came out of his mouth but were no doubt penned by Jabba or one of his mob. He said:

> I completed my medical there (Birmingham). I went back to sign the day after, the paper work wasn't quite ready when I arrived.

During that time the phone call came from here (Neo-Gers).

I was a little bit disappointed it sort of turned sour and the fact that I 'failed a medical' because I have actually got the email confirmation from the club to my agents.

I don't really want to comment on it too much but I never failed a medical, I completed everything that was asked for.

The paper work was supposed to be ready and it got delayed until the next day - that's when the phone call came in.[19]

Of course, he couldn't turn down the chance to play at Ibrox, could he? As he put it: 'There's getting to the Premier League then after that there's obviously the attraction of the Champions League. It's up to us now to get there.'[20]

So there we had it. He had signed to the Ibrox club so he could play in the Champions League. Considering he only signed a two-year contract, swaggering out onto the Ibrox pitch to the strains of 'Zadok the Priest' was going to be a pretty tall order. But, then, he's so used to cramming everything in that time has probably lost all meaning.

Warburton talked the lad up, saying how he loved football so much that 'whenever you speak to Rob it's like Christmas morning, he just wants to play football, always has done'.[21] He probably thought all his Christmases had come at once when he was asked to sign for Neo-Gers at a rumoured five grand a week![22] Warburton also played the Level 5 game, saying that Kiernan had 'had offers to go back down into the Championship'.[23] All that was missing was the usual story about Celtic missing out on signing him.

With Kiernan's salary and the reported fee of about £200,000[24] paid to Wigan that meant roughly another 1100 season tickets needing to be sold. If Warburton went on at this rate then King's target of 45,000 season books might not be enough. Neo-Gers still had about a dozen duffers left on the books from last season to pay, along with the running costs, electricity bills and the two gardeners. No wonder they were trying to make such a big deal about Warburton and his signings.

Warburton's other target was a far more worrying one than Kiernan. He was looking to get the signature of one John Eustace, a free agent after leaving Derby County. Eustace is another that has played for quite a few clubs in his time, though not as many as Kiernan. He was also a good bit older so he had had time to play for longer at each of his clubs; or, rather, he would have done if he had not been plagued with injury. In fact, he had suffered a knee injury in January 2015 and hadn't kicked a ball in anger since and this probably influenced Derby's decision not to renew his contract, along with the fact that he was getting on a bit, having turned thirty-five in November 2014.

Anyone with a cynical nature might make a damning assessment of Warburton's signings and targets. Of Rob Kiernan, Warburton said, 'I have known him very well from a very young age', while he spoke of Eustace as 'someone I know really well'.[25] Could it be that he was signing up his old pals for a ride on the Ibrox gravy train before it got derailed? Folk might point to Danny Wilson as refutation but the fact was that Wilson was being paid handsomely as well. Time, of course, would tell but Kiernan and Eustace weren't the types to inspire The People with confidence.

18
Problems

I don't know about you but I spend many sleepless nights worrying about how my local bus company is doing. Is Lothian Buses making a profit? Usually one would have to rake through the Financial Times to find such information but the good folk of Inverclyde are luckier; the Daily Record is keeping a watchful eye on their local buses.

On the 19th June the Record let us know that McGill's bus company had doubled its pre-tax profits from £1.75m to £3.2m.[1] Those of us expecting to read about how well, or otherwise, our own local buses were doing over the next few days were to be sorely disappointed. In fact, the article wasn't for the benefit of the denizens of Greenock, Port Glasgow etc. at all. It was for a different audience entirely.

The headline and the opening sentence of the article let us all know at whom it was aimed.

> Bus tycoon brothers James and Sandy Easdale have posted a record £3.2 million profit – just months after their rocky departure from the Rangers FC board.[2]

The rest of the article, meanwhile, had not much to say about the company or why it had made a record profit; it was mostly concerned with Honest Dave's Neo-Gers takeover and how the Easdales had run off before they were forced out.

You could just imagine the members of Sons of Struth etc. reading the headline and shouting, 'Bastards!' The way the article was set out it was as if the profits of McGill's was somehow tied-in with the Easdales' involvement at Ibrox. In reality, the article had nothing much to tell us apart from the bald figures of McGill's turnover and profit. The implication was there, however, for all the hard-of-thinking to absorb.

So even though the Easdales had left Neo-Gers, Level 5 was still doing its best to vilify them and make them look like crooks. The truth was, though, that, love them or hate them, the brothers had been the only ones to take nothing out of the Ibrox club. Neither of them took a salary and any loans they provided were interest-free. Not exactly the behaviour of the 'rats' they were being made out to be, was it?

The big problem with the Easdales was the perception of them. There was no denying that, no matter what their business practices were like, they both looked like everyone's idea of gangsters. Their dress, their hair, their whole demeanour screamed, 'Charles Endell'. They really should have called in Gok Wan or Trinny and Susannah a long time ago!

This was a theme dear to the heart of Bill McMurdo. As he said on his blog:

> Ashley and his businesses are PR disasters. He – and they – fail to communicate effectively with supporters. Supporters are, of course, consumers and when consumers turn on a business, that is when the brown stuff really does hit the fan.[3]

He expanded on this by explaining that Ashley's problem was his secrecy. He was mistrusted at both Neo-Gers and Newcastle because he wouldn't tell the supporters what his plans were. What he needed was exactly the same as what the Easdales needed; a better image in the eyes of the public.

McMurdo was probably right. That was the big problem with Ashley; just when you thought you had him worked out he would do something completely out of the blue that shattered your opinion. He was about as easy to read as a Chinese translation of a James Joyce novel.

Remember Phil Mac Giolla Bhain's theory that Ashley didn't want to run Neo-Gers at all but would be happy with somebody else in charge while he raked in the money from the retail? That made a lot of sense to me and it seemed to be what Ashley wanted, especially when he and his allies abstained from voting at the EGM. It looked as if Phil was right and Ashley was content to let King take over. And then he went and turned things on their head.

What was the point in Ashley demanding his money back? It didn't fit in with the notion that he was going to let Honest Dave run the club. It would also mean a reduction in profits for Sports Direct if King and his cronies were to stump up the £5m. Then again, he could have been calling King's bluff to show that the new board was skint; but, again, what was the point? It just didn't fit with what was expected of him.

And then was the EGM that he called and which he didn't attend. He didn't send anyone either, making the whole thing a waste of time. Instead, he had the meeting with Honest Dave, which again didn't tally with any theory about what he was up to. Certainly he would have been a mug to buy King's shares but why not lend the board more money? Surely that would tighten his grip on Neo-Gers retail? The whole business is getting more and more confusing.

Level 5, meanwhile, ensure that The People, and the rest of us, are kept in the dark as much as possible. The Daily Mail reported on the meeting between Ashley and King, saying that it was just about negotiating the retail contract.[4] Strangely the rest of the media decided to just ignore this story, even though this anodyne version of events doesn't cast King in too bad a light. Jabba and his partners obviously want everyone to steer clear.

This reluctance to even obliquely mention the Daily Mail story shows that there must have been more to the meeting than the Mail made out. If anything, it reinforces what Phil Mac Giolla Bhain said about it. That still leaves us with the problem that the Mail's version makes more sense than the Mac Giolla Bhain one, even though the latter is more likely to be true. So what the hell's going on?

The simple answer is that nobody knows. King's deliberate de-listing from the Stock Exchange means that he's running a private company with nobody knowing what's happening behind closed doors. With Ashley being his usual, inscrutable self, all we're left with is PR spin. This spin, moreover, is all one-sided. Ashley surely must have some kind of PR operating for him but it must be said that they aren't doing a very good job. It's time for something new.

I suggest Mike Ashley calls 07899 947 354 and asks for Jabba. The man showed how mercenary he was back in 2012, announcing the death of Rangers only to argue that it was still alive when Chateau Charlie flashed his chequebook. If billionaire

Ashley was to get in touch with Traynor he'd change sides in a heartbeat!

Speaking of PR, remember the guy that used to hold sway at Ibrox, Jack Irvine, the man that called John Greig 'a bit thick'? There's a character calling himself John James, who posts regularly on the Rangers Supporters Loyal blog and rumours abound that this guy is actually Jack Irvine.

As one wag put it, 'John James has to be Jack Irvine. He's not your usual knuckedragger, as his work is reasonably well written, and actually punctuated.'[5] Whether or not it is Irvine, this John James is no fan of Honest Dave and has plenty to say about the current board.

For example, he states that Halloween Houston, Listy Graham and their ilk were all pretty much bribed by the Real Rangers Men, which means that they are so tied up with the current board that they can't possibly complain about King's regime.[6] This was, apparently, all part of the takeover plan.

> King, Murray & Gilligan did not court Graham, Houston, Chugg etc to gain their support. They courted them to silence them. They knew exactly where the dissent would emanate from when they were exposed as penniless spivs on the make.[7]

Other posts by John James show that this is somebody that isn't just speculating; he seems to have inside knowledge of what's been going on at Ibrox. He also doesn't subscribe to the idiotic belief of the rest of McMurdo's mob that the media are somehow 'anti-Rangers'. In fact, he lists all the main players in the Scottish sports media and claims that they are all Rangers (sic) supporters:

> Keith Jackson played for Rangers under 14s. His colleagues Ralston and Guidi are Rangers supporters. Roddy Forsyth was a shareholder in oldco. Even Graham Spiers is on record as lapsed Rangers supporter. However, if you want fawning look no further than the Herald and Evening Times. Matt Lindsay does not try to conceal his love for our club. Chris Jack seems to be running a Rangers fanzine at The Evening Times. All these so-called journalists are a part of their very own RFC – Rangers Fawning Club.[8]

151

So none of the usual paranoia there; no mention of the 'mhedia' or Celtic running everything. His ideas about silencing any potential opposition are extremely interesting; it was a point most of us missed, even though it was important for anyone taking over at Ibrox. In 'Clash of the Agnivores' my argument was that pretending to be 'still Rangers' left the Neo-Gers board on a hiding to nothing. The People swallowed the Big Lie out of necessity but it led to unforeseen consequences. Since the club was 'still Rangers' then the supporters had unrealistic expectations. Trying to meet these expectations led to money being wasted on highly-paid players to guarantee immediate success, instead of the club building for the future.

Right from the start of the new club, both The People and their friends in the media wanted Real Rangers Men at the top of the marble staircase, in order to give some substance to the Big Lie. Bribing the leaders of the rabble that clamoured for King and his crew was a good way of silencing any unwanted criticism that was bound to appear. The more secure the Big Lie became, the more the expectations of The People would be raised; obviously the Real Rangers Men were aware of this and took appropriate action.

John James, or Jack Irvine, if it is, indeed, he, is, however, guilty of as much spin as Jabba and his merry band. He makes no secret of the fact that he believes that Ashley was the answer to the problems at Ibrox, even though the man hadn't invested so much as a penny. He also has a go at the bedsheet-wavers for chasing off Robert Sarver, a multi-millionaire, who could have turned out to be another saviour.[9]

The reason why the name Robert Sarver had come to the fore again was that he was looking to take over Spanish club Levante. He had the support of the shareholders and had promised to plough £30m into the team.[10] John James and McMurdo's mob treated this story as the equivalent of Jim Bowen saying, 'Let's look at what you could've won!' This, however, was disingenuous.

If you remember, Sarver's proposed deal to Neo-Gers didn't involve any £30m warchests. All Sarver was offering was loans and share issues; the same as everybody else.[11] King was offering a better deal and was going to pack the boardroom with Real Rangers Men. To The People there was no choice to be made. Even in the close season King was still making promises to spend 'Whatever it takes'.[12] The rest of us might laugh but, in reality, The People were stuck with no alternative as far as they could see.

152

So what does your average Neo-Gers supporter have to look forward to? From the looks of things, it's going to be nothing but anguish and heartbreak. Mike Ashley might not be finished with his high-priced lawyer and more court cases could well be forthcoming. He will want his £5m ring-fenced and then there's the little matter of King and his friends driving the share price down.[13] This story is going to keep on running.

And what is the strategy of the bedsheet-wavers to oust Ashley from his position of power? They've called for a boycott of Sports Direct's products, including the replica strips and other Neo-Gers merchandise. Obviously they haven't read the small print of what we already know about Ashley's retail deal. Any unsold merchandise has to be paid for by Neo-Gers at full retail price. And what the hell does the club do with all these jerseys etc.? Perhaps some wee men could walk round Ibrox on match days, shouting, 'Erzi fishell Raynjurz taps! Three furra tenner!'

It just shows the kind of dilemma that The People face these days. Do they buy their kids a new 'Rangers' top and keep giving Ashley their money or boycott and cost the Neo-Gers board a fortune? No matter which way they decide to jump, Ashley's sitting pretty. They'll never get rid of him unless he decides to go.

Meanwhile there's the team to consider. As of the beginning of July Warburton has signed a grand total of three new players, leaving him just a matter of weeks to

get the 'Warburton Revolution' up and running. He's still got a steaming pile of shit left over from last year, all on water-tight contracts and he's given no indication of what he's going to do with them. Are they part of his plans or are they all going to end up in Ally's Garden Centre?

As I write this there has been no movement on the John Eustace front with no indication of whether he's going to sign or not. McMurdo's mob thinks he's looking for some kind of signing-on fee, which is standard practice nowadays.[14] Of course, the Real Rangers Men don't have the money to fork out any fees up front and are relying on season-book sales, ticket sales, broadcasting revenue and, dare I say it, their share of merchandise revenue. No doubt Eustace will get back to them if he doesn't get a better offer.

On June 26th John James claimed that only 12,000 season books had been sold so far.[15] This was some way short of the 45,000 that King was asking The People to fork out for. Money was tight and this was reflected in Warburton's signings and targets for the team.

Jordan Gibson, for example, was a seventeen-year-old player for an amateur side in Worcestershire. There seemed to be some confusion over who he actually played for. The Scottish media claimed that he was signed from Alvechurch FC[16] but, according to the Bromsgrove Standard, he actually played for Bromsgrove Sporting.[17] Whatever team he had played for the lad had had a hard time of it breaking through to the big time, failing at West Bromwich Albion, Stoke City and Wolves. One thing was certain; he was cheap!

Young Jordan hopes to break through into the Neo-Gers first team by Christmas and our media, of course, is painting him as some kind of *wunderkind*. There might be problems on match days as the lad will obviously suffer from the usual teenage traumas. He won't want to go out in front of all those people if he has a big plook on his chin and he'll refuse to get out of his bed on occasion because his girlfriend dumped him. And then he'll make sure he gets red-carded, worried about getting a stauner while sharing the bath or showers with the other players!

Other signing targets are hardly ones to inspire a lot of confidence. Andy Halliday was a development player at Rangers but was let go as he hadn't quite made the grade. He went on to make a name for himself at Livingston but then went down to England, where he scored a couple of important goals but was let go by Bradford City in May 2015. Prior to being released he had missed ten games due to a hamstring injury,[18] which might explain Bradford's reluctance to hold onto him.

Then there's Reece Wabara, who came through Manchester City's academy and signed a three-year deal with the club in 2011. He only ever made one appearance for City, spending most of his time out on loan at Ipswich, Oldham, Blackpool and Doncaster. He signed for Doncaster Rovers permanently in 2014 after being released by Manchester City.

The story given out as to why he left Doncaster in 2015 was that Rovers wanted to keep him but Wabara 'expressed a desire to have a look a little higher.'[19] Strangely, Wabara had something different to say in January 2015.

> There was a bit of interest for this window but I always
> wanted to stay at Doncaster. I love the players and I get
> along really well with the manager. I like the way things are
> going so I wanted to see how the end of the season pans
> out.[20]

Something doesn't quite add up here. So he turned down the chance to play in the English Championship to stay with Doncaster and now he thinks Neo-Gers is a step up? Wabara sustained an injury to his foot in a game against Watford in September 2013. He was given injections to numb the pain so that he could keep playing, but went limping off the field at the end of the following week's match.[21] Incredibly, he continued to play right up until December that year and then was forced to take a few weeks out.[22]

One can't help admiring Wabara's courage but who knows what permanent damage he's done to his foot. Did he have to rely on painkillers during the 2014-2015 season? Everyone's being pretty quiet about it and I would imagine that there's more to Wabara leaving Doncaster than meets the eye. It certainly shows the desperation at Neo-Gers when they're looking to sign somebody without a proper investigation of his history.

Level 5, of course, was spinning enough to make even Rumpelstiltskin's head…well…spin. Wabara was announced as 'Former Manchester City defender', Jordan Gibson was 'former West Brom and Stoke kid', Andy Halliday is always pictured in his glory days at Livingston, while loan target, Harry Winks is a 'highly-rated teenager', even though he's only played for the first team once as a substitute. (Calm down, Mr. Graham; his name's *Winks*. Take your onanistic fantasies elsewhere!)

Despite all this propaganda it seems as if The People are in no hurry to buy season tickets for Ibrox. If there were high levels of sales then we'd soon know about it as the Neo-Gers website and, of course, the Daily Record would be trumpeting it to the skies. Many Neo-Gers supporters are no doubt waiting to see what kind of team Warburton's going to put out, while others appear to be content to pay on a match-by-match basis. They've been fed so much shite over the past three years that surely even they are wary now about what's going to happen next. This, of course, presents Neo-Gers with a huge quandary.

Since Warburton's budget depends entirely on the uptake of season books then low sales means he has nothing to spend. We've already seen how he's trying to build a team on the cheap. Such a team will hardly inspire The People to run out and buy season tickets, leaving Warburton with less and less to spend. It's a vicious circle; low ST sales = cheap signings = low ST sales = cheap signings and so on, round and round. Warburton must be wondering now why the hell he took this job.

Before Warburton's appointment Honest Dave was talking about £30m being invested in the team, with most of it being 'front-loaded' (can't Jabba think of anything new?) to ensure promotion to the Premiership in 2016.[23] So where the hell was it? Surely the 'glib and shameless liar' hadn't been lying?

The truth is fairly obvious; the Real Rangers Men are skint. Everything is being paid on an *ad hoc* basis, with loans from the Three Bears, while King spouts Level 5 pish to try to keep The People mollified. They're going to have to rely on revenue from month to month just to keep the 'Big House' open. And therein lies the rub; although King shouts about wanting 45,000 season books sold, it's really the last thing he wants. Selling practically every seat at Ibrox in one go would be a disaster.

Imagine there were 45,000 season tickets sold; The People would be demanding that a good chunk of this cash be spent on a couple of decent new players. They would have every right to expect this to happen since that is what they were promised. As King well knows, however, throwing millions away in transfer or signing-on fees would leave less money to meet the monthly bills, including the players' wages. There would be very little future income from league matches so Neo-Gers would have to ensure a good run in cup competitions, something that has eluded the club so far. It hardly makes for a great business model, does it?

On the other hand, if the supporters refuse to buy season tickets, King can argue that they are the ones depriving Neo-Gers of the capital needed to actually *buy* players. He's as much as told them this already with his insistence that they are 'co-investors'.[24] Warburton will then have to build a team of 'freebies', whose wages will be paid from revenue from matches at Ibrox. In season 2014-2015 the average attendance was around the 32,000 mark; well down on the previous two years but crowds like that every fortnight would pay the bills and the wages of all those youngsters.

The problems with this model are easy to see. If the team isn't up to much then the crowds go down and there's really no other income stream available. Sponsorship? Forget it. Ashley has everything sewn up and nobody else is getting so much as an A4 poster put up anywhere at Ibrox. The broadcasting money for the whole of Scottish football is pitiful, so Neo-Gers can hardly rely on that. Essentially, there's no money going to be coming in except gate money and, as Phil Mac Giolla Bhain is always telling us, the club has no credit line at a bank. All that will be available will be short-term loans from the Three Bears; and how long can they keep doing that if there's not enough income to pay them back? The only possible way to get money will be to approach Ashley, which, as we have seen, King has already been reduced to doing.

Probably the biggest headache at Ibrox is going to be paying Jabba. The bills are going to be astronomical; those Blythswood Square offices don't come cheap. Considering Level 5 has spent most of its time and energy in pissing off Ashley, then Big Mike isn't going to be overly keen in handing over loans or adjusting the retail contracts in favour of Neo-Gers just so they can hand over the cash to Jabba!

And so the fourth instalment of 'The Journey' begins; although it's really a repeat of the third instalment. With a cheap, thrown-together team, no money, no prospects, no investors, no share issue and Mike Ashley on their back it looks like it's going to be a nightmare season for The People. Still, they got what they wanted, didn't they? There are Real Rangers Men in charge and a FIFA magazine article said that their club is 'still Rangers'. Life couldn't be better.

Be afraid, Timmy

157

NOTES

Introduction – Pretty Vacant

[1] Daily Mail 1-11-14
[2] Daily Record 4-11-14

Chapter 1 God Save The Queen

[1] http://therangersreport.com/2014/05/05/is-charlie-telfer-on-verge-of-signing-with-dundee-united/
[2] ibid
[3] http://www.bbc.co.uk/sport/0/football/27672711
[4] http://www.dailyrecord.co.uk/sport/football/football-news/kenny-miller-quits-canada-third-3497106
[5] ibid
[6] http://therangersreport.com/2014/05/09/what-went-wrong-for-kenny-miller-in-vancouver/
[7] http://www.bbc.co.uk/sport/0/football/27793911
[8] http://www.bbc.co.uk/sport/0/football/27756109
[9] http://www.dailyrecord.co.uk/sport/football/football-news/rangers-chief-graham-wallace-insists-3664536
[10] http://www.bbc.co.uk/sport/0/football/27828992
[11] http://www.dailyrecord.co.uk/sport/football/football-news/rangers-directors-hold-showdown-talks-3668192
[12] ibid
[13] http://www.bbc.co.uk/sport/0/football/27793911
[14] http://metro.co.uk/2014/06/15/why-next-seasons-scottish-championship-will-be-one-of-the-more-exciting-leagues-4757029/
[15] http://provenquality.com/scottish-championship-201415-division/
[16] http://worldsoccertalk.com/2014/06/08/with-hearts-hibs-and-rangers-next-seasons-scottish-championship-will-be-mouthwatering/
[17] http://www.scotzine.com/2014/07/will-rangers-walk-away-with-the-scottish-championship/
[18] http://www.edinburghnews.scotsman.com/sport/football/hearts/hearts-sell-more-season-tickets-than-last-year-1-3476754
[19] http://www.edinburghnews.scotsman.com/sport/football/hearts/season-ticket-prices-reduced-at-hearts-1-3441521
[20] http://www.bbc.co.uk/sport/0/football/28134315
[21] ibid
[22] http://www.dailyrecord.co.uk/sport/local-sport/sons-season-tickets-selling-like-3808324
[23] http://www.falkirkfc.co.uk/season-ticket-rallying-call-from-houston/

[24]http://www.raithrovers.net/14837/rovers-smash-season-ticket-sales-record.htm

[25]http://www.alloaadvertiser.com/sport/alloaathletic/articles/2014/05/29/499592-alloa-season-tickets-in-high-demand-ahead-of-historic-season-in-spfl-championship/

[26]http://www.raithrovers.net/14837/rovers-smash-season-ticket-sales-record.htm

[27] ibid

[28] http://www.bbc.co.uk/sport/0/football/27854157

[29]https://billmcmurdo.wordpress.com/2014/06/16/weans-world/

[30]http://www.rangers.co.uk/news/headlines/item/6988-gers-confirm-pre-season-tours

[31]http://www.eveningtimes.co.uk/commonwealth-games/cwg-legacy/a-new-beginning-for-glasgow-s-east-end.1373640275

[32]https://www.whatdotheyknow.com/request/how_much_is_being_spent_on_ibrox#incoming-497212

[33]https://billmcmurdo.wordpress.com/2014/07/16/the-games-people-play/

[34] ibid

[35] ibid

[36] Ibid

Chapter 2 I'm Not Your Stepping Stone

[1] http://spfl.co.uk/challenge-cup/fixture/3636394/

[2]http://www.dailyrecord.co.uk/sport/football/football-match-reports/pictures-rangers-beat-hibs-2-1-3996385

[3]http://www.edinburghnews.scotsman.com/sport/football/hibs/verdict-from-ibrox-handling-the-highs-and-lows-1-3500462

[4] http://www.bbc.co.uk/sport/0/football/28678687

[5] ibid

[6] http://www.bbc.co.uk/sport/0/football/28647379

[7] http://www.bbc.co.uk/sport/0/football/28734145

[8] http://www.bbc.co.uk/sport/0/football/28713408

[9]http://www.dailyrecord.co.uk/sport/football/football-news/rangers-boss-ally-mccoist-points-4034438

[10]http://www.dailyrecord.co.uk/sport/football/football-news/keith-jackson-rangers-on-field-struggles-4034765

[11]http://www.dailymail.co.uk/sport/football/article-2738117/Rangers-brink-tycoon-Dave-King-refuses-underwrite-4m-share-issue.html

[12]http://www.eveningtimes.co.uk/rangers/u/rangers-fans-fears-over-renaming-of-ibrox.1408308917

[13]https://billmcmurdo.wordpress.com/2014/02/26/kicking-tyres/

[14]http://www.dailyrecord.co.uk/sport/football/rangers-big-interview-keith-

jackson-4161076

[15] https://billmcmurdo.wordpress.com/2014/09/06/we-need-a-billionaire-a-fan-speaks-out/

[16] http://www.theguardian.com/business/2006/nov/04/retail

[17] http://www.telegraph.co.uk/finance/comment/richardfletcher/5051922/JJB-deal-shows-sports-retailing-is-not-cricket.html

[18] http://www.theguardian.com/business/2006/nov/04/retail

[19] ibid

[20] ibid

[21] http://www.managementtoday.co.uk/news/1152855/JJB-Sports-blows-whistle-133-stores/

[22] http://www.managementtoday.co.uk/news/937849/Police-raid-Sports-Direct-JJB-blows-whistle/

[23] http://www.proactiveinvestors.co.uk/companies/news/8017/serious-fraud-office-investigates-jjb-and-sports-direct-for-suspected-price-fixing-8017.html

[24] http://www.telegraph.co.uk/finance/newsbysector/retailandconsumer/11289876/Former-JJB-chief-Chris-Ronnie-jailed-for-four-years.html

[25] http://www.chroniclelive.co.uk/sport/football/football-news/newcastle-united-officially-one-worlds-8493633

[26] https://billmcmurdo.wordpress.com/2014/09/08/the-right-man-at-the-wrong-time/

[27] http://www.dailyrecord.co.uk/sport/football/rangers-big-interview-keith-jackson-4161076

[28] ibid

[29] ibid

[30] http://www.dailyrecord.co.uk/sport/football/prospective-rangers-owner-mike-ashley-4161063

[31] http://www.philmacgiollabhain.ie/the-name-game/

[32] http://www.dailyrecord.co.uk/sport/football/football-news/sports-hotline-live-rangers-fans-4163264

[33] http://www.dailyrecord.co.uk/sport/football/football-news/rangers-fans-fury-mike-ashley-4167651

[34] ibid

[35] ibid

Chapter 3 My Way

[1] http://www.dailyrecord.co.uk/sport/football/football-news/rangers-stave-immediate-threat-administration-4249865

[2] ibid

[3] http://www.eveningtimes.co.uk/rangers/union-of-fans-threaten-ibrox-board-agm-mayhem-after-rangers-share-180353n.25313795

[4] https://billmcmurdo.wordpress.com/2014/09/12/all-to-pay-for/

5 http://www.bbc.co.uk/sport/0/football/29446152

6 http://www.bbc.co.uk/sport/0/football/29464478

7 ibid

8http://www.telegraph.co.uk/sport/football/teams/rangers/11137078/Mike-Ashleys-possible-takeover-of-Rangers-moves-one-step-closer-after-he-buys-more-shares.html

9https://billmcmurdo.wordpress.com/2014/09/11/ashley-and-rangers/

10http://www.theguardian.com/football/2014/sep/12/mike-ashley-newcastle-selling

11 ibid

12http://www.dailyrecord.co.uk/sport/football/football-match-reports/alloa-1-rangers-1-david-4297574

13http://www.dailyrecord.co.uk/sport/football/football-match-reports/rangers-1-hibs-3-first-half-4348762

14http://www.scotzine.com/2014/10/mike-ashley-calls-for-removal-of-graham-wallace-and-philip-nash/

15 ibid

16http://www.dailyrecord.co.uk/sport/football/football-news/dave-king-confident-deal-can-4439859

17 ibid

18 http://www.philmacgiollabhain.ie/a-serious-man/

19http://www.football365.com/scottish-football/9568874/Rangers-chairman-David-Somers-says-Dave-King-offer-did-not-meet-due-diligence-requirements

20http://www.dailyrecord.co.uk/sport/football/football-news/mike-ashley-demanded-ownership-rangers-4404886

21http://www.dailyrecord.co.uk/sport/football/football-news/rangers-power-battle-mike-ashley-4499365

22 http://www.bbc.co.uk/sport/0/football/17364884

23 http://www.bbc.co.uk/sport/0/football/30123149

24 ibid

25http://www.dailymail.co.uk/sport/football/article-2807256/Brian-Kennedy-tries-thwart-Mike-Ashley-s-control-Scottish-club-Rangers.html

26 Ibid

27http://www.scotsman.com/sport/football/spfl-lower-divisions/rangers-board-to-consider-brian-kennedy-loan-offer-1-3583243

28 ibid

29https://billmcmurdo.wordpress.com/2014/10/27/its-over-to-you-super/

30http://www.telegraph.co.uk/sport/football/teams/rangers/11131196/Rangers-fans-group-Sons-of-Struth-threaten-boycott-of-Mike-Ashleys-Sports-Direct-shops.html

31 ibid

32http://www.dailymail.co.uk/sport/football/article-2789354/furious-rangers-fans-staged-angry-protest-against-mike-ashley-s-increasing-influence-sports-direct-stores.html

[33] https://www.facebook.com/SonsOfStruth/posts/1538173936413729

[34] http://www.dailyrecord.co.uk/sport/football/football-news/rangers-supporters-trust-take-mike-4539453

[35] ibid

[36] http://www.fleshershaugh.com/

[37] http://www.redandblackshirt.com/#buy

[38] http://www.rangersmegastore.com/puma-rangers-home-shirt-2014-2015-long-sleeve-377429?colcode=37742921

[39] http://www.rangersmegastore.com/puma-rangers-third-shirt-2013-2014-mens-379539?colcode=37953944

[40] http://www.vanguardbears.co.uk/statement-on-the-rfff-committee.html

[41] 'Clash of the Agnivores', Chapter 25

[42] http://blogs.channel4.com/alex-thomsons-view/davc-king-deserve-chance-rangers/8819

Chapter 4 No Feelings

[1] http://www.premierleague.com/en-gb/clubs/profile.stadium.html/newcastle

[2] https://billmcmurdo.wordpress.com/2014/09/06/we-need-a-billionaire-a-fan-speaks-out/

[3] ibid

[4] http://www.philmacgiollabhain.ie/the-sevco-experiment/#more-5748

[5] http://www.dailyrecord.co.uk/sport/football/football-news/rangers-power-battle-how-mike-4527461

[6] http://www.oldham-chronicle.co.uk/news-features/10/oldham-athletic-news/86668/boundary-park-name-change-in-1m-deal

[7] http://www.philmacgiollabhain.ie/the-sevco-experiment/#more-5748

[8] http://www.dailymail.co.uk/sport/football/article-2796183/newcastle-running-life-s-gas-magpies-owner-mike-ashley.html

[9] http://www.dailymail.co.uk/sport/football/article-2588429/Dave-King-commit-30m-ensure-Rangers-return-Scottish-Premiership.html

[10] http://www1.skysports.com/football/news/11788/9561052/scottish-football-mike-ashley-has-provided-another-1631m-loan-to-rangers

[11] http://www.dailyrecord.co.uk/sport/football/football-news/rangers-appoint-derek-llambias-non-executive-4556907

[12] ibid

[13] http://www.dailyrecord.co.uk/sport/football/gordon-waddell-rangers-players-shrug-4678381

[14] ibid

[15] http://www.friendsofrangers.co.uk/1806.html

[16] http://www.bbc.co.uk/news/uk-scotland-glasgow-west-23587678

[17] http://www.heraldscotland.com/sport/football/slow-death-as-rangers-legends-leave.26133619

Chapter 5 Liar

[1] http://news.bbc.co.uk/sport1/hi/football/teams/r/rangers/9161213.stm

[2] http://www.telegraph.co.uk/sport/football/teams/rangers/9329513/Rangers-in-crisis-SFA-asks-Fifa-to-rule-on-status-of-newco-players.html

[3] http://www.outlaw.com/en/topics/employment/business-sales-and-outsourcing/basic-guide-to-tupe/

[4] http://www.independent.co.uk/sport/football/scottish/neil-alexander-to-leave-rangers-as-ally-mccoist-searches-for-new-goalkeeper-8673173.html

[5] http://www.express.co.uk/sport/football/449240/EXCLUSIVE-Neil-Alexander-launches-Ibrox-legal-fight

[6] ibid

[7] http://www.dailyrecord.co.uk/sport/football/football-news/neil-alexander-wins-84k-compensation-4825598

[8] http://sport.stv.tv/football/clubs/rangers/303747-scottish-fa-to-hear-appeal-as-neil-alexander-wins-84000-from-rangers/

[9] http://www.dailyrecord.co.uk/sport/football/football-news/neil-alexander-wins-84k-compensation-4825598

[10] http://forum.rangersmedia.co.uk/index.php?showtopic=277154

[11] ibid

[12] ibid

[13] ibid

[14] ibid

[15] http://www.eveningtelegraph.co.uk/sport/dundee-united/dundee-united-chairman-no-change-in-transfer-for-charlie-telfer-1.680667

[16] http://sport.stv.tv/football/clubs/rangers/302861-dundee-united-ordered-to-pay-rangers-170000-for-charlie-telfer-move/

[17] http://www.dailyrecord.co.uk/sport/football/football-news/rangers-forced-u-turn-charlie-telfer-4778953

[18] ibid

[19] http://sport.stv.tv/football/clubs/rangers/303123-rangers-oldco-liquidators-seek-chunk-of-charlie-telfer-tribunal-cash/

[20] http://www.philmacgiollabhain.ie/a-big-house-divided-3/

[21] http://www.bbc.co.uk/sport/0/football/30340965

[22] http://www.dailymail.co.uk/sport/football/article-2874180/Ally-McCoist-resigns-Rangers-manager-salary-increase-750-000-enters-12-month-notice-period.html

[23] http://www.dailyrecord.co.uk/sport/football/football-news/ally-mccoist-reasons-behind-rangers-4842819

[24] ibid

[25] http://www.philmacgiollabhain.ie/i-can-vouch-for-this/

[26] http://www.eveningtimes.co.uk/rangers/rangers-legend-derek-johnstone-

urges-board-not-to-bow-to-fan-pressure-191232n.26039328

[27]http://www.dailyrecord.co.uk/sport/football/football-news/keith-jackson-ally-mccoist-wont-4750781

[28]http://www.ibroxnoise.co.uk/2014/12/ally-mccoist-master-manipulator.html

[29]http://www.dailyrecord.co.uk/sport/football/football-news/ally-mccoist-reasons-behind-rangers-4842819

[30]http://www.theguardian.com/football/2014/dec/21/ally-mccoist-rangers-gardening-leave

Chapter 6 No Fun

[1]http://www.dailyrecord.co.uk/sport/football/football-news/rangers-agm-its-fans-fault-4851937

[2] ibid

[3] https://www.youtube.com/watch?v=NzU17H9yTl8

[4]http://www1.skysports.com/football/news/11788/9617321/rangers-agm-members-of-board-heckled-at-fiery-agm-at-ibrox

[5]http://www.dailyrecord.co.uk/sport/football/football-news/video-scum-rats-stooges--4853565

[6] ibid

[7]http://www.rangers.co.uk/news/headlines/item/8273-result-of-agm

[8]http://www.dailyrecord.co.uk/sport/football/football-news/video-scum-rats-stooges--4853565

[9]http://www.scottishfa.co.uk/scottish_fa_news.cfm?page=2986&newsID=14110&newsCategoryID=1

[10]https://billmcmurdo.wordpress.com/2014/12/16/the-bucks-start-here/

[11] ibid

[12] 'Clash of the Agnivores', Chapter 23

[13]http://news.stv.tv/west-central/299521-european-commission-dismiss-allegations-celtic-were-granted-state-aid/

[14]https://billmcmurdo.wordpress.com/2014/11/14/the-national-sport-and-the-way-forward/

[15]https://footballtaxhavens.wordpress.com/2014/12/17/audit-scotland-investigating-corruption-involving-the-celtic-sla-at-the-lennoxtown-initiative/

[16]http://news.stv.tv/west-central/303818-rangers-ordered-to-pay-250000-oldco-ebt-commission-fine-by-spfl/

[17]http://www.theguardian.com/football/2014/dec/17/rangers-appeal-spfl-250000-fine

[18]http://news.stv.tv/west-central/303818-rangers-ordered-to-pay-250000-oldco-ebt-commission-fine-by-spfl/

[19]http://www.theguardian.com/football/2014/dec/17/rangers-appeal-spfl-250000-fine

[20]http://www.brentfordfc.co.uk/news/article/brentford-sign-lewis-macleod-from-rangers-2175178.aspx
[21]http://www.dailyrecord.co.uk/sport/football/football-news/rangers-power-struggle-laxey-partners-4898356
[22] ibid

Chapter 7 Did You No Wrong

[1]http://www.express.co.uk/sport/football/549969/Rangers-Dave-King-Ibrox-Rangers-Shares
[2] http://www.thetakeoverpanel.org.uk/
[3] http://www.bbc.co.uk/sport/0/football/30661103
[4]http://www.theguardian.com/football/2010/dec/21/alisher-usmanov-arsenal-stake
[5] http://www.bbc.co.uk/sport/0/football/30661103
[6] ibid
[7]http://www.scotsman.com/sport/football/spfl-lower-divisions/lewis-macleod-i-didn-t-want-to-leave-rangers-1-3656926
[8]http://www.dailyrecord.co.uk/sport/football/for-every-10-spent-retail-4730464
[9]http://www.scotsman.com/sport/football/spfl-lower-divisions/rangers-bid-robert-sarver-denies-mike-ashley-link-1-3654648
[10]http://www.scotsman.com/sport/football/spfl-lower-divisions/rangers-bid-robert-sarver-denies-mike-ashley-link-1-3654648
[11]http://www.dailyrecord.co.uk/sport/football/football-news/rangers-power-struggle-robert-sarver-4924645
[12]http://www.bbc.co.uk/sport/0/football/30678270
[13]http://www1.skysports.com/football/news/11788/9645014/rangers-to-go-to-arbitration-after-sfa-upholds-163250000-ebt-penalty
[14]http://www.dailymail.co.uk/sport/football/article-2806494/Premier-League-hi-vis-winter-ball-set-used-time-weekend.html
[15]http://www.dailymail.co.uk/sport/football/article-2913899/Rangers-vs-Hearts-abandoned-just-25-minutes-snow-home-fans-protest.html
[16] Ibid
[17]http://www.edinburghnews.scotsman.com/news/jambos-attacked-as-snow-halts-ibrox-match-1-3664386
[18]http://www.dailyrecord.co.uk/sport/football/football-news/rangers-caretaker-boss-kenny-mcdowall-5007133
[19]http://www.dailymail.co.uk/sport/football/article-2913641/Rangers-supporters-group-reject-Mike-Ashley-s-plans-Ibrox-Stadium.html
[20]http://www.telegraph.co.uk/sport/football/teams/rangers/11352369/Rangers-fans-break-into-stadium-offices-in-protest-after-match-with-Hearts-is-abandoned.html

21https://billmcmurdo.wordpress.com/2015/01/17/no-comment-required/
22 ibid
23http://www.express.co.uk/sport/football/552557/Dave-King-s-call-Ex-director-hopes-EGM-will-let-him-oust-Rangers-board
24http://www.dailyrecord.co.uk/sport/football/football-news/jack-irvine-paul-murrays-more-5015233
25http://www.endole.co.uk/company/SC494998/level5pr-ltd
26 http://level5pr.co.uk/aboutus/
27 http://level5pr.co.uk/testimonials/
28http://level5pr.co.uk/ourservices/
29 http://level5pr.co.uk/testimonials/
30 ibid
31http://www.snspix.com/04-02-15-lcvel-5pr-press-conference/photo/122676.html
32http://www.scotsman.com/news/odd/charles-green-horse-ibrox-comes-8th-in-debut-race-1-3622421
33http://www.dailyrecord.co.uk/sport/football/football-news/ex-rangers-chief-executive-charles-green-4737228
34http://paddyontherailway12.blogspot.co.uk/2014/12/the-boys-frae-alloa.html
35http://forum.rangersmedia.co.uk/index.php?showtopic=278630
36https://billmcmurdo.wordpress.com/2015/01/20/charles-green-arrest-fairy-tale/
37 https://www.youtube.com/watch?v=-vVSzSfw2TU
38http://www.dailyrecord.co.uk/sport/football/football-news/rangers-crisis-charles-green-gives-5011017
39 ibid
40 http://www.bbc.co.uk/sport/0/football/31010900
41 ibid
42 Ibid

Chapter 8 Silly Thing

1http://www.dailyrecord.co.uk/sport/football/football-news/scottish-league-cup-draw-old-4549250
2 ibid
3 ibid
4http://www.dailyrecord.co.uk/news/crime/rookie-police-taught-sectarian-songs-5057746
5http://www.theguardian.com/society/2015/jan/30/glasgow-police-domestic-abuse-old-firm-rangers-celtic
6https://billmcmurdo.wordpress.com/2015/01/30/conspiracies-and-certificates-old-firm-2015/
7http://babb.telegraph.co.uk/2015/01/celtic-fans-take-out-full-page-advert-

disputing-the-history-of-the-club-currently-playing-out-of-ibrox/

[8]http://www.scotsman.com/sport/football/spfl-lower-divisions/rangers-legends-slam-celtic-fans-newspaper-advert-1-3670540

[9]http://roblufc.org/2015/01/30/celtic-fans-open-to-ridicule-over-rangers-old-firm-claims-by-rob-atkinson/

[10] ibid

[11]https://photobhoy.wordpress.com/2015/03/06/eastern-rovers-a-precursor-to-celtic-fc/

[12]http://www.scotsman.com/sport/football/spfl-lower-divisions/rangers-legends-slam-celtic-fans-newspaper-advert-1-3670540

[13]http://news.bbc.co.uk/sport1/hi/football/europe/3554530.stm

[14]http://www.heraldscotland.com/news/home-news/celtic-coachs-green-and-white-welcome-for-bottle-attack-boy-kieran.117946376

[15]http://www.dailyrecord.co.uk/news/scottish-news/young-rangers-fan-injured-bottle-5119825

[16]http://www.heraldscotland.com/news/home-news/celtic-coachs-green-and-white-welcome-for-bottle-attack-boy-kieran.117946376

[17]http://willievass.photoshelter.com/gallery-image/080215-Rangers-v-RaithRovers/G0000.iy2qRLPmnY/I0000PKteDLJacI8/C00006DiGYgk8MHY

[18]http://www.dailyrecord.co.uk/news/scottish-news/celtic-fan-launches-fund-collect-5096783

[19]http://www.dailyrecord.co.uk/news/local-news/rutherglen-businessman-keep-doubling-reward-5138211

[20]http://www.dailyrecord.co.uk/sport/football/football-news/spfl-chiefs-wait-three-separate-5092740

[21]http://sport.stv.tv/football/clubs/celtic/310528-no-action-to-be-taken-by-spfl-over-old-firm-sectarian-songs-and-banner/

[22]http://www.dailyrecord.co.uk/sport/football/football-news/kenny-miller-gulf-between-celtic-5087389

[23]http://www.dailymail.co.uk/sport/football/article-2936378/Rangers-taken-bigger-Old-Firm-beating-Celtic-Hampden-pitch-better.html

Chapter 9 Bodies

[1]http://www.theguardian.com/football/blog/2015/feb/03/rangers-newcastle-five-loan-players-mike-ashley

[2]http://www.dailyrecord.co.uk/sport/football/football-transfer-news/rangers-sign-five-newcastle-fringe-5095617

[3] http://www.bbc.co.uk/sport/0/football/31079381

[4]http://www.telegraph.co.uk/sport/football/teams/rangers/11399590/Raith-Rovers-leave-Rangers-down-and-out.html

[5]http://www.dailymail.co.uk/sport/football/article-2944864/Rangers-1-2-Raith-Rovers-Gers-stunned-knocked-Scottish-Cup-Newcastle-loanees-

make-debuts.html
[6]http://www.telegraph.co.uk/sport/football/teams/rangers/11396950/Rangers-move-EGM-410-miles-from-Ibrox-to-London-to-avoid-angry-fans.html

[7]http://www.dailymail.co.uk/sport/football/article-2946712/Rangers-board-seek-new-London-venue-club-s-EGM-disruption-fears.html

[8]http://www.dailyrecord.co.uk/sport/football/football-news/egm-held-ibrox-say-rangers-5180018

[9] ibid

[10]http://www.telegraph.co.uk/sport/football/teams/rangers/11418623/Rangers-directors-to-hold-EGM-at-Ibrox-and-not-London-after-all.html

[11]http://www.dailyrecord.co.uk/sport/football/football-news/former-rangers-director-paul-murray-5011803

[12]http://www.dailymail.co.uk/sport/football/article-2943432/Dave-King-s-credentials-attacked-Rangers-board-club-schedule-March-EGM.html

[13] ibid

[14] ibid

[15] http://www.bbc.co.uk/sport/0/football/31367566

[16]http://www.dailyrecord.co.uk/sport/football/football-match-reports/rangers-0-hibernian-2-easter-5160921

[17] ibid

[18] http://www.bbc.co.uk/sport/0/football/23498276

Chapter 10 Belsen Was A Gas

[1]http://www.dailyrecord.co.uk/sport/football/football-news/stan-collymore-take-rangers-tv-5191313

[2] ibid

[3]http://www.dailyrecord.co.uk/opinion/sport/euan-mclean-stan-collymore-bigot-5199835

[4]http://www.dailyrecord.co.uk/sport/football/football-news/rangers-fans-hit-back-stan-5193620

[5]http://www.dailyrecord.co.uk/opinion/sport/euan-mclean-stan-collymore-bigot-5199835

[6] http://nilbymouth.org/resources/history/

[7] ibid

[8] http://nilbymouth.org/resources/history/

[9]http://www.dailyrecord.co.uk/sport/football/football-news/rangers-fans-hit-

back-stan-5193620

[10]http://www.mirror.co.uk/sport/football/news/stan-collymore-dropped-pundit-bt-5195275

[11]http://www.heraldscotland.com/news/home-news/bt-sport-stan-collymore-does-not-want-to-work-for-us-anymore-over-rangers-row.119005182

[12]http://www.dailystar.co.uk/news/latest-news/426779/Sacked-football-pundit-Stan-Collymore-demands-Paul-Gascoigne-banned-TV

[13]http://www.theguardian.com/football/blog/2015/feb/21/debate-old-firm-rangers-celtic

[14]http://www.dailyrecord.co.uk/opinion/sport/euan-mclean-stan-collymore-bigot-5199835

[15]http://www.scotsman.com/news/scotland/top-stories/glasgow-2014-clyde-mascots-stolen-vandalised-1-3502640

[16]http://www.dailyrecord.co.uk/opinion/sport/euan-mclean-stan-collymore-bigot-5199835

[17] ibid

[18]http://www.dailyrecord.co.uk/sport/football/football-news/rangers-fans-hit-back-stan-5193620

[19]https://answers.yahoo.com/question/index?qid=20081019042920AAaTdeL

[20]http://www.scotzine.com/2012/12/fran-sandaza-interview-opens-up-old-wounds-of-sectarianism/

[21]http://theredevilspot.blogspot.co.uk/2010/11/chicharito-to-ditch-his-pre-match.html

[22]http://www.dailyrecord.co.uk/sport/football/football-news/rangers-deny-telling-fran-sandaza-1508161

[23]   https://billmcmurdo.wordpress.com/2014/01/10/when-two-tribes-go-to-war/

[24]   https://billmcmurdo.wordpress.com/2013/07/08/british-glory-scotlands-shame/

[25]http://www.dailyrecord.co.uk/sport/football/isnt-there-enough-to-worry-about-without-beating-991268

Chapter 11 You Need Hands

[1]http://www.dailyrecord.co.uk/sport/football/football-news/daily-records-gary-ralston-beats-5160989

[2]http://www.dailyrecord.co.uk/sport/football/football-news/rangers-board-slap-ban-daily-5135276

[3] ibid

[4]http://www.dailyrecord.co.uk/sport/football/football-news/rangers-director-james-easdale-resigns-5225877

[5]http://www.dailyrecord.co.uk/sport/football/football-news/rangers-chairman-david-somers-officially-5256839

[6]http://www.dailyrecord.co.uk/sport/football/football-news/minister-unleashes-hell-rangers-directors-5255585

[7] ibid

[8] ibid

[9]http://www.dailyrecord.co.uk/sport/football/football-news/rangers-egm-recap-dave-king-5283460

[10] http://www.bbc.co.uk/sport/0/football/31759573

[11]http://willievass.photoshelter.com/gallery/100315-Rangers-v-QOS/G0000P14eR3.oW9U/C0000ULY86euRIRg

[12] ibid

[13] http://www.bbc.co.uk/sport/0/football/31704676

[14]http://www.scotsman.com/sport/football/english/stuart-mccall-lifts-lid-on-rangers-loan-players-1-3724730

[15] ibid

[16]http://www.eveningtimes.co.uk/rangers/mbabu-keen-to-get-started-at-rangers-as-he-recovers-from-injury-196965n.118219125

[17]http://www.dailyrecord.co.uk/sport/football/football-news/rangers-loanee-gael-bigirimana-knew-5400265

[18] http://www.bbc.co.uk/sport/0/football/31839589

[19]http://www.dailyrecord.co.uk/sport/football/football-news/stuart-mccall-leaves-motherwell-manager-4555664

[20]http://www1.skysports.com/football/news/11788/9612275/spfl-stuart-mccall-tight-lipped-on-rangers-job

[21]http://www.talkingbaws.com/2014/12/12/5-managers-who-could-replace-ally-mccoist-as-rangers-boss/

[22] http://www.bbc.co.uk/sport/0/football/31893214

[23]http://www.dailyrecord.co.uk/sport/football/football-match-reports/hibernian-0-rangers-2-gers-5381076

[24]http://rangers.co.uk/match/match-reports/2014-15/item/8930-rangers-4-1-cowdenbeath

[25]http://www.heraldscotland.com/news/home-news/rangers-llambias-easdale-and-leach-suspended.1425990566

[26]http://www.dailyrecord.co.uk/sport/football/football-news/rangers-chiefs-make-three-more-5305856

[27]http://www.heraldscotland.com/news/home-news/rangers-llambias-easdale-and-leach-suspended.1425990566

[28]http://www.dailyrecord.co.uk/news/scottish-news/chris-graham-muslim-leaders-demand-5322152

[29]http://www.theguardian.com/football/2015/mar/13/chris-graham-resign-rangers-director-prophet-muhammad-star-wars

[30]http://www.dailyrecord.co.uk/news/scottish-news/former-rangers-director-chris-graham-5330579

[31] ibid

[32] Ibid

Chapter 12 Something Else

1 http://www.dailyrecord.co.uk/sport/football/football-news/rangers-shares-suspended-after-wh-5272779

2 http://sport.stv.tv/football/clubs/rangers/312774-dave-king-insists-he-has-a-nomad-lined-up-ahead-of-rangers-takeover/

3 http://www.scotzine.com/2015/03/thy-king-dom-come-at-rangers/

4 http://www.philmacgiollabhain.ie/buyers-remorse/

5 http://www.dailyrecord.co.uk/sport/football/football-news/video-keith-jackson-financial-wrecking-5363311

6 http://www.gersnetonline.co.uk/vb/showthread.php?69508-Keith-Jackson-Discusses-Rangers-Collapse-at-2015-Money-in-Sport-Conference

7 ibid

8 http://www.ibroxnoise.co.uk/2015/03/do-rangers-need-to-be-on-stock-exchange.html

9 http://www.dailymail.co.uk/sport/football/article-2981954/Rangers-Q-Dave-King-reveals-money-come-new-chairman-turn-Ibrox-around.html

10 http://www1.skysports.com/football/news/11788/9746560/dave-king-and-his-consortium-have-won-control-of-rangers

11 http://www.dailyrecord.co.uk/sport/football/football-news/keith-jackson-new-rangers-boards-5426016

12 http://www.express.co.uk/sport/football/561971/Dave-King-blasts-Rangers-nomad

13 http://www.dailyrecord.co.uk/sport/football/football-news/keith-jackson-new-rangers-boards-5426016

14 http://sport.stv.tv/football/clubs/rangers/315947-rangers-delisted-from-stock-exchange-after-failing-to-find-new-adviser/

15 http://www.bbc.co.uk/sport/0/football/32164350

16 http://www.welbeckassociates.com/resources/tips-succeeding/business/floating-aim-or-isdx-markets

17 http://www.dafferns.com/news/accounts/do-private-companies-still-need-to-hold-an-agm-by-martin-gibbs/

18 http://www.heraldscotland.com/news/home-news/rangers-agree-emergency-15m-loan-with-three-bears.1427120216

19 http://www1.skysports.com/football/news/11788/9746560/dave-king-and-his-consortium-have-won-control-of-rangers

20 http://www.dailyrecord.co.uk/sport/football/football-news/rangers-chairman-paul-murray-dave-5416432

21 http://www.ibroxnoise.co.uk/2015/03/do-rangers-need-to-be-on-stock-exchange.html

22 ibid

23 http://www.bbc.co.uk/sport/0/football/32099753

24 ibid
25 http://www.bbc.co.uk/sport/0/football/32088535
26http://www.dailymail.co.uk/sport/football/article-3032656/Queen-South-3-
0-Rangers-Derek-Lyle-Lewis-Kidd-Gavin-Reilly-strike.html

Chapter 13 Watcha Gonna Do About It?

1http://www.dailyrecord.co.uk/sport/football/football-news/rangers-pay-
newcastle-united-500000-5432370
2http://www.dailyrecord.co.uk/sport/football/football-news/rangers-board-
launches-probe-after-5487885
3http://news.stv.tv/west-central/316649-rangers-badges-transferred-to-mike-
ashley-as-security-for-5m-loan-deal/
4 http://www.bbc.co.uk/sport/0/football/32089210
5 http://www.bbc.co.uk/sport/0/football/30963740
6 http://www.bbc.co.uk/sport/0/football/32325215
7http://www.dailyrecord.co.uk/sport/football/football-news/spfl-bow-
pressure-switch-hearts-5528778
8http://forum.rangersmedia.co.uk/index.php?showtopic=282471
9http://www.dailyrecord.co.uk/sport/football/football-news/stuart-mccall-
calls-rangers-boo-5584789
10http://www.rangers.co.uk/match/match-reports/2014-15/item/9142-rangers-
2-2-falkirk
11 http://www.bbc.co.uk/sport/0/football/32363664
12http://www.heraldscotland.com/sport/football/rangers-2-falkirk-2-mccalls-
anger-at-mcculloch-boos.124301576
13http://www.falkirkherald.co.uk/sport/falkirk-fc/rangers-2-falkirk-2-bairns-
denied-history-1-3754401
14 http://www.bbc.co.uk/sport/0/football/32319194
15http://www.scotsman.com/sport/football/spfl-lower-divisions/hibs-hearts-
and-well-call-for-more-play-off-cash-1-3745377
16http://www.dailyrecord.co.uk/sport/football/football-news/hibs-bid-grab-
more-premiership-5569435
17http://www.dailymail.co.uk/sport/football/article-3039213/Hibernian-face-
battle-lower-league-clubs-gate-revenue-lucrative-play-ties-Rangers-
Motherwell.html
18http://sport.stv.tv/football/clubs/hibernian/317251-hibernian-bid-to-keep-
bigger-share-of-premiership-play-off-gate-receipts/
19http://www.hibernianfc.co.uk/news/5352
20http://www.dailyrecord.co.uk/sport/football/football-news/hibs-bid-grab-
more-premiership-5569435
21http://www.dailyrecord.co.uk/sport/football/football-news/cash-strapped-
rangers-set-hand-spfl-5478355

22 http://www.bbc.co.uk/sport/0/football/32425392

23http://www.eveningtimes.co.uk/rangers/murray-blasts-former-board-for-rangers-stock-market-woes-202325n.122359819

24 http://www.philmacgiollabhain.ie/hurry-and-wait/

25http://www.philmacgiollabhain.ie/sevco-salaries-in-april/

26http://www.dailyrecord.co.uk/sport/football/football-news/rangers-collision-course-spfl-play-off-5600337

27https://rangerssupportersloyal.wordpress.com/2015/04/24/no-isdx-for-rangers/#comments

28 ibid

29 ibid

30http://www.dailyrecord.co.uk/sport/football/football-news/record-football-show-watch-top-5601940

31http://www.edinburghnews.scotsman.com/sport/football/hibs/hibs-hands-tied-against-free-entry-to-play-offs-1-3767846

32http://www.sundaypost.com/sport/football/rangers-boss-stuart-mccall-calls-for-a-yellow-cards-amnesty-1.865919

33http://www.dailyrecord.co.uk/sport/football/football-news/rangers-charge-fans-just-fiver-5652084

34 ibid

35http://www.eveningtimes.co.uk/rangers/rangers-set-to-sell-out-ibrox-for-play-off-rematch-with-queen-of-the-206407n.125767819

36 ibid

37   http://www.dailymail.co.uk/sport/football/article-3079545/Mike-Ashley-demands-Rangers-extraordinary-meeting-Newcastle-owner-seeks-recoup-5m-loan.html

38   http://www.dailyrecord.co.uk/sport/football/football-news/mike-ashley-goes-war-rangers-5687137

39 http://www.dailyrecord.co.uk/sport/sons-struth-plea-rangers-fans-5570264

40http://www.dailyrecord.co.uk/sport/football/football-news/rangers-takeover-probe-police-raid-5642669

41http://www.philmacgiollabhain.ie/a-strange-kind-of-raid/

42   http://www.dailyrecord.co.uk/sport/football/football-news/youre-no-oil-painting-rangers-5682145

43http://www.dailyrecord.co.uk/sport/football/football-news/rangers-u-turn-sees-embarrassing-new-5683817

44 ibid

Chapter 14 Anarchy in the UK

1http://www.dailyrecord.co.uk/sport/football/football-news/keith-jackson-seems-like-fate-5715992

2http://www.dailyrecord.co.uk/opinion/sport/record-fc-hibernian-ticket-farce-

5695312

3http://www.dailyrecord.co.uk/sport/football/football-news/dave-king-allowed-become-chairman-5692550

4http://www.dailyrecord.co.uk/sport/football/football-news/stuart-mccall-urges-rangers-fans-5724875

5 http://www.bbc.co.uk/sport/0/football/32775770

6http://www.dailyrecord.co.uk/opinion/sport/record-fc-hibernian-missile-throwing-5742352

7 ibid

8http://dothebouncy.com/main/threads/the-official-d-t-b-rangers-fc-vs-hibernian-fc-match-thread.65435/page-6

9http://www.dailyrecord.co.uk/opinion/sport/record-fc-hibernian-missile-throwing-5742352

10 ibid

11http://www.theguardian.com/football/2015/may/22/dave-king-confirmed-chairman-rangers-sfa

12http://www.rangers.co.uk/news/headlines/item/9346-king-appointed-chairman

13 ibid

14http://www.telegraph.co.uk/sport/football/teams/rangers/11626687/Rangers-appoint-John-Greig-as-honorary-life-president.html

15 http://www.bbc.co.uk/sport/0/football/32775776

16   http://www.dailyrecord.co.uk/sport/football/football-news/hibs-boss-alan-stubbs-blasts-5751560

17http://www.dailyrecord.co.uk/sport/football/football-news/rangers-announce-general-meeting-promise-5767026

18 Ibid

Chapter 15 Don't Give Me No Lip, Child

1http://www.telegraph.co.uk/sport/football/teams/rangers/11626687/Rangers-appoint-John-Greig-as-honorary-life-president.html

2http://www.dailyrecord.co.uk/sport/football/football-news/richard-foster-play-offs-favour-5765997

3 ibid

4 ibid

5http://www.dailyrecord.co.uk/sport/football/football-news/no-one-likes--dont-5775596#rlabs=1

6 ibid

7http://www.pieandbovril.com/forum/index.php/topic/223164-motherwell-v-hibs-rangers-play-off-final/page-3

8http://dothebouncy.com/main/threads/the-official-d-t-b-rangers-fc-vs-motherwell-fc-match-thread.65552/

[9] http://www.dailyrecord.co.uk/sport/football/football-news/rangers-handed-just-1500-tickets-5763049
[10] http://www.dailyrecord.co.uk/sport/football/football-news/stuart-mccall-fir-park-ticket-5771059
[11] http://www.dailyrecord.co.uk/sport/football/football-news/rangers-handed-just-1500-tickets-5763049
[12] http://www.dailyrecord.co.uk/sport/football/football-news/empty-seats-fir-park-make-5772252
[13] http://www1.skysports.com/football/news/11781/9865116/rangers-restricted-to-1500-for-scottish-premiership-play-off-final-against-motherwell
[14] http://www.dailyrecord.co.uk/sport/football/football-news/rangers-1-motherwell-3-recap-5779491
[15] http://www.theguardian.com/football/2015/may/28/rangers-motherwell-scottish-premiership-play-off-final-first-leg
[16] http://www.dailyrecord.co.uk/sport/football/football-news/rangers-1-motherwell-3-recap-5779491
[17] http://www.dailyrecord.co.uk/sport/football/football-news/kris-boyd-set-rangers-sos-5789044
[18] Ibid
[19] http://www.dailyrecord.co.uk/sport/football/football-match-reports/motherwell-3-rangers-o-recap-5796745
[20] http://www.scotsman.com/sport/football/spfl/punch-sparks-shameful-scenes-at-play-off-final-1-3788879
[21] http://www.eveningtimes.co.uk/rangers/bilel-mohsni-faces-boot-from-rangers-after-shameful-fir-park-brawl-208694n.127608073
[22] http://www.dailyrecord.co.uk/opinion/sport/gary-ralston-couple-minutes-fir-5799302
[23] http://www.dailyrecord.co.uk/opinion/sport/david-mccarthy-rangers-supporters-deserve-5810709
[24] https://www.youtube.com/watch?v=xmuODjMPuXU
[25] http://www.dailyrecord.co.uk/opinion/sport/gary-ralston-couple-minutes-fir-5799302
[26] http://www.dailyrecord.co.uk/sport/football/football-news/mum-bad-boy-ranger-bilel-mohsni-5805843

Chapter 16 No One Is Innocent

[1] https://rangerssupportersloyal.wordpress.com/2015/05/21/268/#comments
[2] ibid
[3] http://www.dailyrecord.co.uk/sport/football/football-news/rangers-board-ready-war-after-5768552
[4] http://www.dailyrecord.co.uk/sport/football/football-news/fifa-insist-rangers-same-football-5752723

[5]http://www.eveningtimes.co.uk/rangers/u/fifa-step-into-new-row-over-rangers-old-or-new-club-status.1432476546

[6] http://de.wikipedia.org/wiki/Peter_Eggenberger_(Autor)

[7]http://www.dailymail.co.uk/news/article-3098633/Swiss-police-arrest-ten-FIFA-officials-allegations-corruption-involving-World-Cup-bids-broadcast-deals-gather-Zurich-elect-new-president.html

[8] ibid

[9] http://www.philmacgiollabhain.ie/questions-about-rangers-in-europe/

[10] http://maleysbhoys.com/2012/06/02/campbell-ogilvie-a-suitable-president-of-the-scottish-football-association/

[11]http://www.express.co.uk/sport/football/467110/Campbell-Ogilvie-to-fight-for-FIFA-role

[12] http://www.bbc.co.uk/sport/0/football/33063657

[13]http://videocelts.com/2015/03/blogs/latest-news/uefa-snub-ogilvies-executive-committee-bid

[14]http://www.dailyrecord.co.uk/sport/football/football-news/campbell-ogilvie-replaced-sfa-president-5851574

[15] http://www.onfieldsofgreen.com/no-resolution/

Chapter 17 C'Mon Everybody

[1]http://www.dailyrecord.co.uk/sport/football/football-news/dave-king-urges-rangers-fans-5849000

[2]https://en.wikipedia.org/wiki/2012%E2%80%9313_Rangers_F.C._season

[3]http://www.dailyrecord.co.uk/sport/football/football-news/dave-king-urges-rangers-fans-5849000

[4] ibid

[5] ibid

[6] ibid

[7] http://www.rangers.co.uk/news/headlines/item/9465-dave-king-renewal-letter

[8]http://www.dailymail.co.uk/sport/football/article-2591251/Dave-King-My-father-anti-football-didnt-want-Rangers-fan.html

[9] ibid

[10]http://www.rangers.co.uk/news/headlines/item/9465-dave-king-renewal-letter

[11]http://www.telegraph.co.uk/sport/football/teams/rangers/11669493/Mike-Ashley-wins-Rangers-gagging-order.html

[12]http://www.eveningtimes.co.uk/news/13332540.Mike_Ashley_s_gagging_order_on_Rangers_extended_to_Scotland/

[13]http://www.philmacgiollabhain.ie/dave-king-offered-his-shares-to-ashley-at-meeting-on-june-12th/#more-6487

[14]https://rangerssupportersloyal.wordpress.com/2015/06/14/infighting-

between-fans-on-social-media/#comments

[15]http://www.dailyrecord.co.uk/sport/football/football-news/daily-record-football-show-new-5885646

[16]http://www.dailyrecord.co.uk/sport/football/football-news/new-rangers-signing-danny-wilson-5935761

[17]https://www.facebook.com/TheRangersFootballClubLtd?ref=stream&hc_location=stream

[18]http://www.birmingham.vitalfootball.co.uk/article.asp?a=403013

[19]http://www.birminghammail.co.uk/sport/football/football-news/birmingham-city-rob-kiernan-lifts-9512379

[20] ibid

[21]http://www.dailyrecord.co.uk/sport/football/football-news/rangers-boss-mark-warburton-new-5934311

[22]https://www.facebook.com/TheRangersFootballClubLtd?ref=stream&hc_location=stream

[23]http://www.dailyrecord.co.uk/sport/football/football-news/rangers-boss-mark-warburton-new-5934311

[24]http://www.manchestereveningnews.co.uk/sport/football/football-news/rob-kiernan-follows-james-mcclean-9514653

[25]http://www.dailyrecord.co.uk/sport/football/football-news/danny-wilson-becomes-mark-warburtons-5930692

Chapter 18 Problems

[1]http://www.dailyrecord.co.uk/news/scottish-news/james-sandy-easdale-post-record-5912166

[2] ibid

[3] https://billmcmurdo.wordpress.com/2015/04/

[4]http://www.dailymail.co.uk/sport/football/article-3136746/Rangers-chairman-Dave-King-holds-secret-talks-bid-ease-Mike-Ashley-s-grip-retail-deal.html

[5] http://kerrydalestreet.co.uk/topic/9240021/196/

[6]https://rangerssupportersloyal.wordpress.com/2015/06/26/rsl-statement/#comments

[7] ibid

[8]https://rangerssupportersloyal.wordpress.com/2015/06/25/spin-on-this/#comments

[9]https://rangerssupportersloyal.wordpress.com/2015/06/26/rsl-statement/#comments

[10]http://www.dailyrecord.co.uk/sport/football/football-news/phoenix-knight-robert-sarver-hand-5951147

[11]http://www.dailyrecord.co.uk/sport/football/football-news/rangers-put-robert-sarvers-20million-4939376

[12]https://www.pressandjournal.co.uk/fp/sport/football/spfl/604245/king-promises-rangers-will-spend-big-to-secure-the-title/

[13]http://www.philmacgiollabhain.ie/sevco-confidential/

[14]https://rangerssupportersloyal.wordpress.com/2015/06/26/rsl-statement/#comments

[15]https://rangerssupportersloyal.wordpress.com/2015/06/25/spin-on-this/#comments

[16]http://www.dailyrecord.co.uk/sport/football/former-manchester-city-defender-reece-5964321

[17]http://bromsgrovestandard.co.uk/sport/teenager-gibson-makes-dream-move-to-rangers-10572/

[18]http://www.thetelegraphandargus.co.uk/sport/12963743.Bradford_City_unlikely_to_bank_on Halliday/

[19]http://www.dailyrecord.co.uk/sport/football/football-news/mark-warburton-steps-up-rangers-5966825

[20]http://www.doncasterfreepress.co.uk/sport/doncaster-rovers/reece-wabara-snubs-championship-interest-to-stay-at-doncaster-rovers-1-7027621

[21]http://www.thestar.co.uk/sport/football/doncaster/doncaster-rovers-no-pain-no-gain-for-on-loan-manchester-city-defender-reece-wabara-1-6083673

[22]   http://www.doncasterroversfc.co.uk/news/article/wabara-injury-update-post-scan-1212221.aspx

[23]http://www.dailyrecord.co.uk/sport/football/football-news/dave-king-well-spend-whatever-5846790

[24] http://www.rangers.co.uk/tickets/season-tickets

44139863R00115

Printed in Poland
by Amazon Fulfillment
Poland Sp. z o.o., Wrocław